# Deacons and Vatican II

# Deacons and Vatican II

## The Making of a Servant Church

Michael J. Tkacik

WIPF & STOCK · Eugene, Oregon

DEACONS AND VATICAN II
The Making of a Servant Church

Wipf & Stock
An Imprint of Wipf and Stock Publishers
199 W. 8th Ave., Suite 3
Eugene, OR 97401

www.wipfandstock.com

PAPERBACK ISBN: 978-1-5326-4819-9
HARDCOVER ISBN: 978-1-5326-4820-5
EBOOK ISBN: 978-1-5326-4821-2

Manufactured in the U.S.A.

To Suzy,
the Prophetess,
who, on a daily basis,
witnesses *kenosis* and *diakonia*
unto me

# Contents

# Acknowledgments

OVER THE COURSE OF my twenty-five years of full-time university-level teaching I have been abundantly blessed, personally and professionally, by the opportunities which I have been afforded by a number of dioceses to share in the formation and journey of a plethora of deacon candidates and their wives. This book is an expression of my gratitude to and affection for them in light of all that they have done for me as I have grown in my own spiritual journey. I particularly wish to acknowledge the 2008 Deacon Class of the Diocese of Savannah, Georgia ("The Dead Theologians Society") and the 2012 Deacon Class of the Diocese of Richmond, Virginia—two groups with which I became particularly close and which edified my personal and professional life in profound ways.

The aforesaid opportunities would not have been possible if not for the commitment to collaborate offered to me and my host institution, Saint Leo University, by the Deacon Directors of the Dioceses of Savannah, Georgia, Orlando, Florida, and St. Petersburg, Florida—Deacons George Foster (Savannah), Bob Kinsey (of blessed memory) and Marshall Gibbs (Orlando), and John Alvarez (St. Petersburg). My thanks to them for entrusting me with a small portion of the formation process of their candidates and for becoming my friends and spiritual brothers.

Teaching deacon candidates and their wives on weekends in distant dioceses meant that I had to frequently be away from my home and family—missing many little league games and other family events. My thanks, therefore, are also extended to my wife,

# ACKNOWLEDGMENTS

Suzy, and to my three sons, Charles, Benjamin and Samuel—
thank you for so generously sharing me and supporting me even
when doing so may have come at a cost to you. An additional
thanks to Suzy for her help in editing, preparing and readying the
book for publication.

# 1

# The Ecclesiology of the Second Vatican Council and the Restoration of the Permanent Diaconate

> The best preparation for the new millennium can only be expressed in a renewed commitment to apply, as faithfully as possible, the teachings of Vatican II to the life of every individual and to the whole Church. (Pope John Paul II, *Tertio Millennio Adveniente* #20, 1994)

## Ecclesial *Aggiornamento* and the Diaconate

THE WORDS OF THE late Pope John Paul II noted above bespeak of the late pope's confidence in the Second Vatican Council and the hope that the council holds for the church as it strives to convey the ongoing relevance and viability of the gospel message to the modern world. Animated and guided by the prophetic vision of the pope who convened the Second Vatican Council, Pope John XXIII, the council committed the church to pastoral engagement with the modern world via a dialectic of mutual exchange between the church and the world. Pope John lamented that the church had come to be viewed as a type of museum housing relics of antiquity. To overcome such a perception, Pope John called for the church to open its windows and undertake a spring cleaning via which the church, in turn, would reform, modify, adapt, update, reform and renew itself via a process of *aggiornamento*. Pope John longed for the church to engage the modern world in a mutual dialectic so as to discern more effective ways and means for the church to communicate the perennial meaningfulness and relevance of the gospel.

> It is equally necessary for the Church to keep up to date with the changing conditions of this modern world, and of modern living, for these have opened up entirely new avenues for the Catholic apostolate. (Pope John XXIII's opening address of the Second Vatican Council)

Pope John's attitude and disposition towards the modern world was one of optimism. The rapidly changing world was not something that the church ought to fear, reject or retreat from. Rather, the changes within the modern world presented the church with new possibilities for immersing (incarnating) itself within the world and new ways for the church to serve the world. The church's task, according to Pope John, was to preserve the immutable truths and values of the gospel (what we will call big-"T" Truths—immutable gospel Truths/Values), yet communicate these Truths/Values in a manner that resonated with and that were intelligible to the modern world (what we will call little-"t" truths—ecclesial formulations/expressions/communications of gospel Truths/Values).

> What is needed is that this certain and immutable doctrine . . . be studied afresh and reformulated in contemporary terms. For this deposit of faith, or truths which are contained in our time-honored teaching is one thing; the manner in which these truths are set forth is something else . . . We must work out ways and means of expounding these truths in a manner more consistent with a predominantly pastoral view of the Church's teaching office. (Pope John XXIII's opening address of the Second Vatican Council)

While the world changes, the Truths and Values of the gospel endure. However, the ways and means by which the church conveys these Truths and Values of the gospel must change so as to adapt to and effectively address the changing pastoral needs of human beings. The Second Vatican Council committed itself to this task of rendering the Truths and Values of the gospel meaningful and viable to modern humanity.

> With the help of the Holy Spirit, it is the task of the en-tire People of God, especially pastors and theologians, to hear, distinguish and interpret the many voices of our age, and to judge them in the light of the divine word, so that revealed truth can always be more deeply pen-etrated, better understood and set forth. (*Gaudium et Spes* #44)

Following the example of the fledgling Christian movement/church as described in the Book of Acts—empowered by the Holy Spirit the early community of believers were able to go forth and universally engage the world so as to ensure the spread of the gospel to all peoples—the Second Vatican Council identified en-gagement with the world and the lives of the faithful as one of the principal tasks confronting the contemporary church, as accentu-ated by the council's recognition that the church, by its very nature, is missionary (*Ad Gentes* #2). The council was committed to Pope John XXIII's call for *aggiornamento* and to reading the signs of the times so as to interpret them in light of the gospel.

> At all times the Church carries the responsibility of read-ing the signs of the times and interpreting them in the light of the Gospel. (*Gaudium et Spes* #4)

Such efforts to demonstrate the ongoing relevance and viability of the church vis-à-vis the modern world requires that the church reform itself in ways and means that better enable it to incarnate itself within the various cultural contexts of humanity and that better enable it to reveal how the gospel addresses contemporary anthropological, social, economic and political realities. Just as the primitive church, as presented in Acts, sought to engage the world with the gospel—via the apostles at Pentecost (the apostles emerge from hiding to go forth and undo Babel via universal evangeliza-tion); saints Stephen and Philip (early "deacons" who preserved tradition, confronted the religious establishment and extended the gospel message to outsiders); Peter (via his encounter with Cornelius) and Paul (via his extensive travels and missions unto the Gentiles); etc.—the seminal and longest document promulgated by the Second Vatican Council, *Gaudium et Spes* (*The Pastoral Constitution on the Church in the Modern World*), was devoted to precisely these self-same aims.

Toward these ends, the Second Vatican Council called for the restoration of the permanent diaconate.

> ... it will be possible in the future to restore the diaconate as a proper and permanent rank of the hierarchy. (*Lumen Gentium* #29)

> It is the task of the legitimate assemblies of bishops of episcopal conferences to discuss ... whether and where—in view of the good of the faithful—the diaconate is to be instituted as a proper and permanent rank of the hierarchy. (Pope Paul VI, *Sacrum Diaconauts Ordinem*, 1967)

As was the case with the earliest expressions of diaconal ministry, as recorded in the Book of Acts, the restored permanent diaconate was deemed by the council members to be a necessary and useful ministry within the church, particularly for facilitating conversation regarding the pastoral needs of the community between the faithful and their ecclesial leaders, and for ecclesial ministries of public service. (Acts 6 presents the Greek-speaking members of the faith community expressing their pastoral concerns to the apostles. The apostles, in turn, charge the community with selecting seven ministers to serve the community's pastoral needs. Once selected, the community presents the seven ministers to the apostles who, in turn, accept them via the laying on of hands). Given the objectives of collegial and communal ecclesial inter-relationships and engagement with the world set forth for the church by the Second Vatican Council, the council members drew upon this ministry depicted in the Book of Acts by calling for the restoration of the permanent diaconate as a means by which the modern church and its leadership might better connect with the faithful and address their pastoral needs. As Paul McPartlan explains, "by being visibly at home in both the church and the world the deacon embodies the great message of Vatican II."[1] Therefore:

> The restoration of the permanent diaconate should surely be seen as an integral part of the Council's work of preparing the whole church for a renewed apostolate in today's world . . . Deacons are animators of service so as to help form a servant-church.[2]

The restoration of the permanent diaconate, itself, is an example of the Second Vatican Council's commitment to *aggiornamento*. In the words of the late Pope John Paul II:

> A deeply felt need in the decision to re-establish the permanent diaconate was and is that of greater and more direct presence of Church ministers in the various spheres of the family, work, school, etc., in addition to existing pastoral structures. ("Deacons Serve the Kingdom of God" #6, 1993)

## The Diaconate and Ecclesial Efforts to Read the Signs of the Times

The restoration of the permanent diaconate by the Second Vatican Council flowed forth from the wider ecclesiological vision of the council which accentuated the church at the service of the world thereby incarnating the gospel and infusing the secular/temporal realm with the spirit of Christ.

> Deacons . . . should be conversant with contemporary cultures and with the aspirations and problems of their times . . . In this context, indeed, the deacon is called to be a living sign of Christ the Servant and to assume the church's responsibility of reading the signs of the time and interpreting them in light of the Gospel. (Congregation for the Clergy, *Directory* #43, 1998)

1. McPartlan, "Deacon and *Gaudium et Spes*," 67.
2. Ibid., 72.

Given the trifold focus of diaconal ministry—liturgy, word and charity—the deacon sacramentally embodies the church-world dialectic at the heart of the Second Vatican Council's ecclesiological vision. Furthermore, by participating in holy orders with accompanying active involvement in the sacramental and evangelical economies of the church, as well as having a particular charism unto facilitating the church's apostolate of justice/service unto the world while also being a member of a family and secular worker, the deacon possesses unique spiritual gifts and a unique vocational identity which enable the deacon to sacramentally exemplify the church-world interconnection. Given the Second Vatican Council's vision of the church at the service of the world, the diaconate, if utilized in a manner consistent with its apostolic past, could do much to serve as the link between the church and world and inspire, animate and facilitate other ecclesial apostolates of service. Pope Paul VI attested to such in *Ad Pascendum*:

> . . . the deacon serves as . . . a mediator of the needs and desires of Christian communities, an animator of service (of diaconia) of the church among the local Christian communities, and a sign or sacrament of Christ the Lord Himself.

The deacon is to both express the needs and desires of Christian communities and be a driving force for service (Congregation for Catholic Education, *Basic Norms* #5). From its scriptural origins throughout the apostolic period and up to the Middle Ages, the deacon has not only been consistently associated with *ad intra* ecclesial liturgical functions, but has also been a member of the church hierarchy entrusted with managing communal finances and the community's *ad extra* apostolates of service, charity and justice, as well as an episcopal representative and informant on matters pertaining to the lived experiences of the faithful. The deacon-bishop relationship is pertinent to our consideration for the deacon was deemed to be the bishop's ear, mouth, heart and soul, i.e., the bishop's chief administrator and principal advisor regarding the needs of the community (see the *Didascalia Apostolorum*). Given the deacon's responsibilities and relationship to the bishop, deacons regularly succeeded their bishops to the episcopacy. This relationship between deacon and bishop was even more pronounced in the church of Rome given the bishop of Rome's stature within the universal church. Rome preserved the scriptural precedent of keeping seven deacons and seven archdeacons. As key advisors of the pope, deacons wielded much authority within the Roman Church—this is particularly evident in the third century subsequent to the Gnostic challenge and prior to the Constantinian Revolution, as demonstrated by Pope Fabian's alignment of the church of Rome into seven districts overseen by the deacons (a structure that persisted through the eleventh century), and the relationship between St. Lawrence and Pope Sixtus II—in face of persecution and martyrdom at the hands of the emperor Valerian the pope entrusted the church and its riches to Lawrence, his deacon.

As noted above, the Book of Acts presents Saints Stephen and Philip as having roles within the apostolic community by which they ascertained the needs of the faithful, presented them to the apostles, and returned to the community of believers to implement the apostolic faith. Additionally, both Stephen and Philip had an authority in their own right that enabled them to recount the tradition vis-à-vis religious authorities, and to make pastoral decisions deemed appropriate for the spread of the faith among disparate communities.

In addition to the aforesaid testimony and witness of Scripture and third-century examples, there is a chorus of consistent presentations of the diaconate in early church writings. The *Didache*, *Shepherd of Hermas*, Clement of Rome, Ignatius of Antioch, Polycarp, Justin Martyr, Tertullian, *Didascalia Apostolorum*, Hippolytus and Cyprian each and all testify to the communal and sacramental roles of the deacon, ranging from communal and financial oversight to Eucharistic assistance, baptizing and hearing confessions, to apostolates of justice, to episcopal assistance, to type of Christ, etc.[3] As early as the third century, and as late as the

---

3. See Ditewig, *Emerging Diaconate*, 43–78; Enright, "History of the Diaconate"; and Ditewig, "Kenotic Leadership of Deacons."

eleventh century, archdeacons exercised extensive and authoritative ecclesial oversight, including advisor to and representative of the bishop, caretaker of church monies and of the poor, overseer of other clergy and their selection, formation and appointment, and administrator of church property.

In light of these brief overviews of the ecclesiological vision of the Second Vatican Council and the apostolic and historical role of the deacon in the church-world dialectic considered thus far, how might the Second Vatican Council's restoration of the permanent diaconate serve the contemporary church-world dialectic? The Second Vatican Council noted that bishops are the primary shepherds of their dioceses, responsible for the care of the faithful in their charge. So that bishops might better carry out their tasks in ways that are more pastorally effective, the council challenged bishops:

> . . . to strive to become duly acquainted with the laity's needs in the social circumstances in which they live . . . In exercising his pastoral care he should preserve for his faithful the share proper to them in church affairs; he should also recognize their duty and right to collaborate actively in building up the Mystical Body of Christ. (*Christus Dominus* #16)

> He should not refuse to listen to his subjects . . . whom he urges to collaborate readily with . . . (*Lumen Gentium* #27)

The Second Vatican Council also called for institutional ecclesial reforms which facilitate and enable lay participation in the decisions that concern the life and mission of the church:

> Every laymen should openly reveal to them (their bishop) their needs and desires with that freedom and confidence which befits a son of God and brother in Christ . . . let this be done through agencies set up by the church for this purpose . . . Let bishops willingly make use of the laity's prudent advice . . . Attentively in Christ, let them consider with fatherly love the projects, suggestions and desires proposed by the laity. (*Lumen Gentium* #37)

William McKnight, in his reflections on the deacon as mediating figure between the bishop and the faithful, sees the restoration of the permanent diaconate as "an instrument of the Spirit for the growth of the church in service to the Gospel."[4] We echo this sentiment in citing the restoration of the permanent diaconate as what we call a "pneumatic corrective," i.e., fidelity to the directives of the Holy Spirit as revealed to the church through its members which calls upon the church to mirror the *kenosis* of Christ as it empties itself of modalities which no longer serve to address the needs of the faithful and/or restore previous modalities which may, again, serve to address the needs of the faithful by opening itself up to cultural and institutional adaptations and/or restorations which will serve to edify the church.[5]

Part of the challenge facing the contemporary church in its efforts to demonstrate the significance of its message are institutional modifications regarding the exercise of ecclesial authority which bring about, influence and sustain the vision of the Second Vatican Council. This includes taking seriously the lived experience of the laity (*sensus fidelium*) and implementing *ad intra* democratic and participatory forms of governance—forms of governance deemed by the Magisterium to be the most consistent with human dignity (*Octogesima Adveniens* and *Gaudium et Spes* associate such participation and shared governance as an extension of human dignity and *Centesimus Annus* explicitly endorses the principal of subsidiarity and, in principal, democratic forms of governance) and expected of other institutions of power (see Appendix). Therefore, let us take a cue from Kenan Osborne, OFM, as we consider the role of the deacon in the contemporary church:

> Given the variability of early diaconal history and the hiatus of twelve hundred years, we today in our dreams and planning for a third-millennial permanent diaconate need to think creatively, or as the contemporary phrase expresses it, we need to think "outside the box."[6]

4. McKnight, "Diaconate as *Medius Ordo*," 85.

5. See Tkacik and McGonigle, *Pneumatic Correctives*.

6. Osborne, *Permanent Diaconate*, 144.

If we were to fuse the Second Vatican Council's ecclesiological, episcopal and lay apostolate vision with the apostolic vision of the diaconate, we might consider implementing an ecclesial structure which enables deacons to serve as mediators between the laity and bishops in a meaningful and relevant manner. Richard Gaillardetz points out that the deacon is ordained to serve the ministry of the bishops, specifically the bishops' pastoral oversight.[7] Therefore, the deacon can be the one sent forth by the bishop charged with ascertaining the pastoral needs of the faithful and reporting these back to the bishop. Such a mediating role, John Collins notes, captures the apostolic sense of the meaning of deacons as a "go-between" and ambassador—one whose role it is to move back and forth between two parties, relaying messages and acting as a helpful, communicative emissary.[8] Furthermore, William McKnight explains that the intermediary role of the deacon could include representing the bishop's care and concern to the people of God, as well as serve as means by which the laity could participate in decisions which concern the life and mission of the church as called for by the Second Vatican Council. Bill Ditewig further explicates how such a dialectical arrangement of shared decision-making, power and authority rightly sees authority as a communal phenomenon mirroring the *kenotic* example of Jesus. Such a dialectic of authority:

> . . . necessitates intermediate structures to distribute the requisite knowledge for participation . . . By binding the bishop and laity closer together in communion, structures that enhance the bishop's familiarity with the people are a benefit to the church as a whole. The laity, for their part, would be more personally engaged in the life of the church. The bishop, on his part, would receive assistance in making better decisions through the consultation of the expertise and wisdom of the laity . . . the deacon is empowered with special gifts of the Holy Spirit to strengthen the communion of the church by facilitating the relationship between the clergy and the laity . . .

7. See Gaillardetz, "On the Theological Integrity of the Diaconate," 86–88.

8. See Collins, *Deacons and the Church* and *Diakonia*.

> In an age where participation in the decision-making process is perceived as a basic right . . . and distrust of authority figures is growing . . . the pastoral authority of the church could benefit from the service of a sacramental ministry specially designed to communicate the needs and desires of the Christian faithful.[9]

Collectively, these reflections represent nothing other than recovering aspects of the apostolic/patristic model of diaconal ecclesial ministry so as to address contemporary signs of the times and needs of the faithful.

An institutional mechanism/structure conducted by deacons for the sake of facilitating shared dialogue, decision-making, and ecclesial governance between bishops and laity would have a number of advantages:

1. It would promote within the church a system of governance which would mirror the very forms of governance that the church's own teachings associate with the dignity of the human person—participatory, democratic and animated by the spirit of subsidiarity (see Appendix).

2. It would enable bishops to exercise their pastoral leadership and authority in a manner consistent with the teachings of the church—collegially and respectful and receptive of the needs and expertise of the laity.

3. The dignity and baptismal rights and duties of the laity would have a meaningful vehicle/outlet within the institutional/organizational church—exercising their conscience and their prophetic and kingly baptismal charisms.

4. Deacons are sacramentally and pneumatically identified and empowered precisely for such a role as mediator between bishops and the laity, the church and world—via holy orders deacons receive sacramental/pneumatic grace and are bound to the bishop . . . but bound to the bishop in the service and on behalf of the faithful . . . and, frequently, as married men

---

9. McKnight, "Diaconate as *Medius Ordo*," 94–98.

with families and secular jobs, they are able to identify with the experiences of the laity.

5. Communion ecclesiology would be evidenced as bishops came to better know and serve their faithful, and the faithful would gain confidence in and respect for their bishop as pastor and leader.

6. The church's credibility would be enhanced as laity and non-church members would be more likely to embrace the teachings of the church for they would have participated in the decision-making process of the church; and the teachings of the church would be edified due to the contributions of the laity whose expertise in some areas exceeds that of bishops (See *Christus Dominus* #'s 9 and 16).

7. Collectively these advantages would do much to bring to realization the vision of the church afforded us by the Spirit at the Second Vatican Council.

## A New Pentecost: The Second Vatican Council and the Diaconate

Pope John XXIII intuited that the process of ecclesial *aggiornamento* that would characterize the Second Vatican Council would be paramount to a new birth for the church. The pope often referred to "flashes of heavenly light" which illuminated his vision of the council and as it drew nearer he was fond of referring to it as a "New Pentecost!" The pope came to play on the juxtapositioning to Pentecost deliberately for he understood well how it communicated his belief about the exceptional character of the current historical juncture in the life of church—extraordinary prospects lay ahead of the church and, consequently, the church had to renew itself so that it, like the early apostles, would be able to present and explain the gospel message to the world.

> O Holy Spirit, renew your wonders in this our day, as by a new Pentecost. (Pope John XXIII, opening prayer for the Second Vatican Council)

... the Holy Spirit was sent on the day of Pentecost in
order that God might continually sanctify the Church ...
(*Lumen Gentium* #4)

To better appreciate Pope John's sense of the council as a
"New Pentecost" it is helpful to reflect upon the original Pentecost
recorded in the Book of Acts. As the book opens we find the disciples (representative of the early church) gathered around Mary
locked in an attic in fear subsequent to the crucifixion and death
of Jesus. The image is one of the apostles being fearful of the world
and having retreated from the world. The risen Jesus appears to
them and breathes the gift of the Holy Spirit upon them. Upon
receiving the Spirit the apostles (church) are animated and empowered by the Spirit to go forth unto the world so as to perpetuate the message and ministry of Jesus unto all people. The rest of
the book presents the apostles (church) courageously going forth
unto the world to share the gospel (see Acts 2f). The Spirit guides
their efforts. In order to effectively convey the gospel message (Big
"T's") to the myriad of diverse people and pluralistic communities in which they come into contact with, the Spirit illuminates
adaptations whereby the apostles can more effectively present
and convey the gospel (little "t's"), thereby enabling the apostles
(church) to share the Truths and Values of the gospel universally
within varying cultural contexts and to all people. Such was Pope
John XXIII's hope for the modern church as it undertook the
process of *aggiornamento* at the Second Vatican Council. Just as
the original Pentecost marked the birth of the church, Pope John
hoped that the council would, indeed, prove to be a "New Pentecost," i.e., a new birth for the church. And as was the case with
the original Pentecost, the Spirit would animate and empower the
church to overcome its fears of the modern world and engage the
modern world rather than retreat from it. As the church went forth
to engage in a mutual dialectic with the modern world, the pope,
furthermore, foresaw the need for the Spirit to guide the church
in its efforts via illuminating new ways and means for the church
to present the gospel to vastly diverse and pluralistic cultures and
peoples of modern times.

As the Book of Acts narrates the unfolding life of the early church, those exercising diaconal ministry are presented as going forth unto the world empowered by the Spirit to facilitate the spread of the gospel and life of the fledgling church by assisting in the realization and actualization of the charisms of those whom they served in a manner that was inclusive and committed to peace. Via promoting communal justice, effective preaching, interpretation of Scripture, custodial oversight of tradition, inclusivity, missionary efforts and ongoing openness and fidelity to the Holy Spirit, the likes of Saints Stephen and Philip (as well as Saints Peter and Paul) successfully ensured the ongoing intelligibility, viability and longevity of the gospel message. This remains the church's selfsame task today. And, also, today, in the contemporary church, deacons have an indispensable role to play in the church's ongoing efforts to be faithful to the apostolic precedent. Just as diaconal ministry was spawned by the original Pentecost so as to facilitate the church's apostolic mandate, the permanent diaconate was re-established at the "New Pentecost," i.e., the Second Vatican Council, in order to do the same.

## Deacons: Servants of a Servant Church

The Second Vatican Council presented the church as a servant of Christ and, thus, a servant to all humanity.[10]

> The joy and hope, the grief and anguish of the people of our time, especially of those who are poor or afflicted in any way, are the joy and hope, the grief and anguish of the followers of Christ as well. (*Gaudium et Spes* #1)
>
> . . . the Second Vatican Council . . . resolutely addresses . . . the whole of humanity . . . (*Gaudium et Spes* #2)
>
> The church is interested in one thing only—to carry on the work of Christ under the guidance of the Holy Spirit, for he came into the world to bear witness to the

---

10. See Doyle, *Church Emerging from Vatican II*, 248–56.

truth, to save and not to judge, to serve and not to be served. (*Gaudium et Spes* #3)

The council members were inspired and motivated by the commission the church received from Jesus to share the gospel with all people (see Matthew 28:19–20) and the challenge to serve Christ in and through human beings (see Matthew 25:35–46).

Pope John XXIII linked the council with the theme of renewal. Pope John believed that the church was at the threshold of an extraordinarily important historical juncture in which it would be necessary "to define clearly and distinguish between what is sacred in principle and eternal gospel and what belongs rather to the changing times." The pope viewed the current situation as a time in which the church was entering "an age of universal mission, or crossing the line into a new age," therefore it would be necessary for the church to be able to discern "the sign of the times" and be able to recommend how the message of Jesus addresses them (see Pope John XXIII's *Apostolic Constitution Convoking Vatican II, Humanae Salutis*). Furthermore, John XXIII saw the world on the threshold of a new era—secular transformations had brought both technological advancements as well as dangers, particularly the threat of the loss of all sense of the spiritual because moral progress had not kept pace with material progress which lent to a feeling of human independence from God.

> The Church today is witnessing a crisis underway in society. While humanity is at the turning point of a new age, tasks of immense seriousness and size await the Church. (Pope John XXIII, *Humanae Salutis*, English translation)

However, as noted above, such a dire forecast of the modern world did not lead the pope to despair or cynicism, but rather it served to fortify his faith in Christ and the Spirit to utilize the church to feel the rhythm of the time.

> We like to reaffirm our confidence in the Savior who has not left this world which He redeemed. Indeed, we make our own recommendation of Jesus that we know how to distinguish the signs of the times; and we seem to see

> now, in the midst of so much darkness, more than a few
> indications that augur well for the fate of the Church and
> of humanity. (ibid.)

The pope saw the evils and threats of the century as leading people toward more thoughtful and more spiritual values, more eager to work for human integration—thus people were open to the church's teachings.

> In the face of this twofold spectacle—a world which
> reveals a grave state of spiritual need and the church
> of Christ, still so vibrant with vitality—we felt at once
> the urgent duty to call our family together in order to
> enable the Church to contribute more effectively to the
> solution of the problems of the modern age. We expect
> great things indeed from this Council, which wishes to
> reinvigorate faith, doctrine, Church discipline, religious
> and spiritual life; we also expect it to make a great con-
> tribution to the reaffirmation of those principles of the
> Christian order which also inspire and govern develop-
> ments in civic, economic, political and social life. (ibid.)

John XXIII envisioned *ad intra* reform of the church as the means toward the *ad extra* redemption of the modern world. This is why he was so adamant regarding the council's pastoral character, believing that the council would increase charity so as to meet the varied needs of people and present the message of Christ to them more clearly. By embracing the world in such a radical way, the pope was attesting to the fact that the world shares in the process of salvation. Salvation is no longer understood as a phenomenon to be worked strictly *ad intra* the church. The world, too, shares in the process of salvation. For believers, this means that there can be no opposition between our religious life and our social life. For it is in our social existence that we are called to communicate Christ to the world—this is how the church serves as a sacrament of Christ (see *Lumen Gentium* #'s 1, 3, 5, 8–9, 48; *Gaudium et Spes* #'s 21, 24, 27, 39, 42–43, 45, 62; and *Sacrosanctum Concilium* #'s 2, 5, 26). If a dichotomy does exist between these two dimensions of our life then we fail to be church and we contribute to the demise of the world (see *Gaudium et Spes* #19, 43; and *Lumen Gentium* #31).

In his seminal work, *Models of the Church*, Cardinal Avery Dulles expounded upon the notion of church as servant. As servant, Dulles contends, the church must engage in a "secular-dialogic": "secular because the church takes the world as a proper theological locus and seeks to discern the signs of the times; dialogic because it seeks to operate on the frontier between the contemporary world and the Christian tradition."[11] Consequently, Dulles suggests that the church can only be church when it exists for others, working within the structures of the world.

Deacons have a unique and indispensable role to play in the actualization of the church as servant for deacons are icons of Jesus the servant and are the church's service sacramentalized.

> The service of the deacon is the Church's service sacramentalized. Yours is not just one ministry among others, but it is truly meant to be, as Paul VI described it, a "driving force" for the Church's diakonia. By your ordination you are configured to Christ in his servant role. You are also meant to be living signs of the servanthood of his Church. (Pope John Paul II, "Heart of the Diaconate," 1987)
>
> The deacon is a living icon of Christ the servant within the Church. (Congregation for Catholic Education, *Basic Norms* #11)
>
> Deacons are animators of service so as to help form a servant Church.[12]
>
> The vision of Church as servant finds a concrete sacramental expression in the diaconate.[13]

Throughout the rest of the book we will explore how deacons, as icons of Jesus the servant and the church's service sacramentalized, help to bring to realization the Second Vatican Council's vision of the church as servant via:

11. Dulles, *Models of the Church*, 84.
12. McPartlan, "Deacon and *Gaudium et Spes*," 73.
13. Ditewig, "Vatican II and the Renewal of the Diaconate," 119.

Preaching

Teaching

Ministry of Word

Custodianship of tradition

Facilitation of the church's missionary efforts

Informing ecclesial inculturation

Liturgical/Sacramental ministry

Empowering the baptismal dignity of the laity

Promotion of ecumenism and interreligious dialogue

Acting as instruments of peace

Championing human dignity

> We stress that the teaching of the Council is channeled in one direction, the service of humankind . . . The Church has declared herself a servant of humanity . . . the idea of service has been central. (Pope Paul VI, "Homily at the Last General Session of Vatican II")

# 2

# The Second Vatican Council, *Aggiornamento* and Diaconal Ministry

HAVING CONSIDERED THE ECCLESIOLOGICAL vision of the Second Vatican Council and the role that deacons might have in bringing said vision to realization in chapter 1, we now turn our focus to specific ministries exercised by deacons which, if considered in light of the Conciliar task of *aggiornamento*, might prove to enhance the church's efforts to engage the faithful and the modern world in ways and means which reveal the continued relevance and viability of the gospel. More specifically, this chapter will explore how the Second Vatican Council's task of *aggiornamento* impacted and influenced the council's views of preaching, revelation, Scripture, ecclesial teaching and tradition, and how deacons are ably suited to manifest the council's teachings on these matters in ways that resonate with the faithful and that build up the contemporary church.

## Diaconal Preaching

As we have already seen (see chapter 1), the Second Vatican Council wished to update, renew, adapt and reform the church in such ways that ensured the church's ongoing efficacy in presenting the gospel in meaningful and life-giving ways to modern human be-ings. That is, the council committed the church to discovering new ways to present the Truths and Values of the gospel with renewed vigor so as to afford the world a viable encounter with Jesus. Cen-tral to such an evangelical task would be Scripture/the gospel itself for it is via Scripture/the gospel that we encounter the Word (Jesus) within the word (Scripture/gospel). The dynamic encounter with Jesus that the word (Scripture/gospel) affords is facilitated via the action of the Holy Spirit in the process of preaching and interpret-ing the word (Scripture/gospel). As St. Paul expounds:

> And how can they believe in him of whom they have not heard? And how can they hear without someone to preach? And how can people preach unless they are sent? (Romans 10:14–15)

The Second Vatican Council's restoration of the permanent diaconate has yielded the church a wonderful gift, namely a grow-ing number of deacons whose ministry entails the charism of preaching! Proclamation of the word is a ministry directed toward the community for via preaching God's word becomes efficacious as God condescends so as to reveal himself and draw people to himself. The efficacy of God's word derives from its connectedness to he who is the Word of God, Jesus, and the message of salvation he proffers. The preaching of the word renders an effect for it influ-ences the salvation of those who hear it and who encounter the love of God contained within it. The great Catholic theologian Karl Rahner, SJ, is noted for suggesting that preaching can be said to be an exhibitive function, i.e., via the power of the Spirit the preached word renders Jesus the Word available for encounter. Therefore, it follows that if the Second Vatican Council longed for the world to encounter Jesus and his Truths and Values in meaningful, relevant and life-giving ways, then it would be requisitely necessary for the church to be equipped with effective preachers. The Second Vati-can Council's restoration of the permanent diaconate has equipped the church precisely with that. Upon ordination, deacons receive the gospel and are bidden:

> Receive the book of the gospel whose herald you have
> become. Believe what you read. Teach what you believe.
> Practice what you teach. (United States Conference of
> Catholic Bishops, "Rites of Ordination of a Bishop, of
> Priests, and of Deacons." 2003)

As ministers entrusted with preaching, deacons become facilitators of the Spirit-animated dynamic whereby the encounter with the Word within the word is made possible.

> The deacon is ordained to ministry of the Word . . . It is
> properly the role of the deacon to proclaim the Gospel
> . . . because the deacon . . . is a sacramental model that
> exists in the "between" of the Gospel proclaimed and the
> Gospel lived . . .[1]

> This is the very heart of the diaconate to which you have
> been called: to be a servant of the mysteries of Christ . . .
> (Pope John Paul II, "Heart of the Diaconate," 1987)

Therefore, deacons ought to develop their preaching skills earnestly. To effectively facilitate an encounter between Jesus and those to whom the deacon preaches, the deacon must preach the word in a manner intelligible to and readily received by those to whom he preaches.

> . . . it is the first task . . . to preach the Gospel of God to all
> . . . for by the saving Word of God faith is aroused . . . and
> is nourished in the heart of believers . . . Moreover. . . .
> preaching . . . if it is to become more effective in moving
> the minds of its hearers, must expound the Word of God
> . . . by an application of the eternal truth of the Gospel to
> concrete circumstances of life . . . according to the needs
> of the hearers . . . (*Presbyterorum Ordinis* #4)

The deacon, as one whose life mirrors the laity in numerous ways (marriage, family life, work, etc.), is well positioned to do just this. As one who can uniquely identify with and relate to the lived experiences of the faithful, the deacon is, in turn, uniquely positioned to demonstrate to the laity the relevance the gospel holds for their

---

1. Ditewig, *Deacon at Mass*, 66.

lives and thereby facilitate a meaningful and life-giving encounter between them and the Word within the word. In short, deacons are able to help others discern the interconnections between one's faith and one's life.

> Preaching offers a scriptural interpretation of human existence which enables the community to recognize God's active presence, to respond to that presence in faith through liturgical word and gesture, and beyond the liturgical assembly, through a life lived in conformity with the Gospel. (United States Conference of Catholic Bishops, *Fulfilled in Your Hearing* #29, 1982)

Accompanying the deacon's charism of preaching is the explication of the preached word via homilies/sermons which further reveal the enduring Truths and Values of the gospel in a manner that additionally reveals the Word within the word and that illuminates Jesus'/the gospel's ongoing relevance to the faithful's lives.

> The purpose of the homily is to explain the readings and make them relevant for present day. (*Liturgiae Instaurationes* #2a)

> The sermon . . . is the proclamation of God's wonderful works in the history of salvation which is the mystery of Christ ever made present and active in us . . . (*Sacrosanctum Concilium* #35)

> By means of the homily the mysteries of the faith and the guiding principles of the Christian life are expounded . . . (*Sacrosanctum Concilium* #52)

> . . . the homily is a scriptural interpretation of human existence which enables a community to recognize God's active presence, to respond to that presence . . . through a life lived in conformity with the Gospel. (United States Conference of Catholic Bishops, *Fulfilled in Your Hearing* #29, 1982)

Robert P. Waznak, in his *An Introduction to the Homily*, describes how the Second Vatican Council's task of *aggiornamento* informed a renewal of ecclesial homiletics via emphasizing the biblical, liturgical, *kerygmatic*, conversational and prophetic aspects of the homily.[2] Below we will consider how some of these various aspects of the homily identified by the Second Vatican Council can be actualized via diaconal ministry.

## Diaconal Illumination of Revelation and Scripture

As services of the Word via the word, preaching and homiletics must, obviously, be rooted in and informed by Scripture. The Second Vatican Council's application of *aggiornmento* to the church's approach to Scripture is most evidently revealed in the council's *Dogmatic Constitution on Divine Revelation, Dei Verbum.* Beautifully, *Dei Verbum* bespeaks of revelation as God's initiative toward friendship with human beings flowing forth from God's love so as to draw human beings into an intimate relationship with himself (see *Dei Verbum* #2). Furthermore, *Dei Verbum* also bespeaks of the action of the Holy Spirit in the dialectic which occurs between God and human beings via revelation noted above when it bespeaks of the grace and interior assistance that God and the Holy Spirit afford us as we strive to understand revelation (see *Dei Verbum* #5).

> The Holy Spirit constantly perfects faith by His gifts so that revelation may be more and more profoundly understood. (*Dei Verbum* #5)

Succinctly, *Dei Verbum* summarizes God's intentions in revealing Himself:

> . . . God wished to manifest and communicate both Himself and the eternal decrees [Big "T's"] of His will concerning salvation . . . He wished, in other words, to share with us divine benefits . . . (*Dei Verbum* #6)

However, since "God has spoken many times and in various ways" (*Dei Verbum* #4), and in manners befitting of those to whom he was communicating, our understanding of revelation

---

2. See Waznak, *Introduction to the Homily*, 16.

and Scripture "makes progress as we grow in our insights of the realities and words that have been passed on" (*Dei Verbum* #8). With the help of the Holy Spirit we are able to better understand the Truths and Values of the gospel (see *Dei Verbum* #8).

> There is growth in insight into the realities that are being passed on. This comes about in various ways . . . Thus as the centuries go by, the Church is always advancing towards the plenitude of divine truth . . . (*Dei Verbum* #8)

Our enhanced insights and understanding of revelation and Scripture, in turn, are additionally facilitated by applying the tools of the historical-critical method to biblical scholarship. As preachers and homilists, deacons must be well-versed in the historical-critical method of biblical scholarship so as to understand the context and meaning of revelation as understood by those who composed Scripture for:

> The divinely revealed realities which are contained and presented in the text of sacred Scripture have been written down under the inspiration of the Holy Spirit . . . To compose the sacred books God chose certain persons who, all the while He employed them in this task, made full use of their powers and faculties . . . (*Dei Verbum* #11)

So, though God acted in these persons and by them, nevertheless, their unique historical, social, political, and cultural contexts, etc., as well as their unique ingenuity, creativity and vision, colored their respective presentations, i.e., "in sacred scripture God speaks through human beings in human fashion" (*Dei Verbum* #12). Therefore, in their efforts to interpret Scripture and to convey its meaning and relevance to their contemporary audiences, deacons must "ascertain what God wished to communicate to us . . . by carefully searching out the meaning that the sacred authors really had in mind" (*Dei Verbum* #12).

> Seeing that in Sacred Scripture God speaks through human beings in human fashion it follows that the interpreter of Sacred Scripture . . . should carefully search out the meaning which the sacred authors really had in mind

. . . synthesized and explained with an eye toward the situation of the churches . . . (*Dei Verbum* #'s 12 and 19)

Toward this end, deacons must determine the intention of the sacred writers by paying attention to the situations of the communities that they addressed; to the literary forms they utilized; to the determined situation and context, i.e., the particular time and culture of the authors; and to the customary and characteristic perceptions, conventions and patterns of speech which prevailed at the time of authorship (see *Dei Verbum* #'s 17 and 12).

> In determining the intention of the sacred writers attention must be paid to . . . literary forms . . . determining situations and given circumstances of time and culture . . . and customary and characteristic patterns . . . which prevailed at the age of the sacred writer . . . (*Dei Verbum* #12)

In light of the aforesaid, deacons ought to utilize appropriate techniques to examine and explain Scripture in such a way so that as many as possible of those to whom they minister may receive nourishment from Scripture—nourishment that enlightens their minds, strengthens their wills and enflames their hearts (see *Dei Verbum* #23). Consequently, diaconal formation and preparation for preaching and homiletics ought to include education in the areas of biblical exegesis and hermeneutics.

> Diaconal formation must take into account . . . Introduction to sacred Scripture and its authentic interpretation . . . (Unites States Conference of Catholic Bishops, *National Directory* #124a)

The axioms of tradition echoed by the Second Vatican Council's *Dei Verbum* remain sound:

> . . . the study of scripture should be the very soul of sacred theology (*Dei Verbum* #24)

> Ignorance of the Scriptures (word) is ignorance of Christ (Word). (*Dei Verbum* #25)

Therefore:

> The challenge for the deacon is to learn the prayerful art of communicating the faith effectively and integrally to persons in diverse stages of life and in many different cultural circumstances.[3]

Deacons will be better suited to minister unto the Word within the word via their preaching and homiletics if they learn how to discern what the Lord revealed in Scripture and help illuminate this for the assembly of hearers they address.[4]

## Deacons as Teachers

Related to their ministry of the word, deacons, additionally, have an important role to play as teachers of the faith. Again, in light of their unique life stations as well as their unique position within the ecclesial hierarchy and sacrament of holy orders (ordained members of the clergy who also frequently have wives, families and jobs), deacons may prove to be ably suited to teach the faith in a manner more readily intelligible and credible vis-à-vis the faithful if they are able to present the church's teaching in a manner that resonates with the lived experiences of the faithful and is, therefore, deemed credible, received and put into practice.

> . . . a deacon may have a particular advantage in bringing the Church's message to the laity because he lives and works in the secular world. The deacon, because of his familiarity with the day-to-day realities and rhythms of the family, neighborhood and workplace, can relate the rich tradition of Catholic teaching to the practical problems experienced by people (United States Conference of Catholic Bishops, *National Directory* #149)

As trust and confidence in higher levels of the hierarchy have been wounded and, additionally, as the laity have become more educated

---

3. Noll, "Sacramental Ministry of the Deacon," 203.

4. See Untener, *Preaching Better*, 12–14.

in recent years, such credible and effective ecclesial teachers are of paramount importance for the future church.

> An increasingly educated society and the new roles of leadership in diaconal ministry require that a deacon be a knowledgeable and reliable witness to the faith and a spokesman for the Church's teaching. (ibid., #118)

If the teachings of the Second Vatican Council are to be more widely embraced by the faithful and, thus, lend to the greater actualization of the ecclesiological vision of the church as servant unto the world proffered by the council, it follows that effective teaching must be an ecclesial hallmark of the contemporary church. If the council's vision is not taught effectively, it follows that its vision will not be realized. If the council's vision is not realized, then the church's efforts to be a servant unto the world, likewise, will not be realized. For the vision of the Second Vatican Council to be realized, and for the world to be edified by ecclesial demonstration of the ongoing relevance and viability of the gospel, it follows that the faithful must learn this vision and put it into practice. Such a scenario presupposes efficacious ecclesial teaching.

> ... instruction illumines and strengthens the faith, develops a life in harmony with the Spirit of Christ, stimulates a conscious and fervent participation in the liturgical mysteries, and encourages one to take an active part in the apostolate. (*Gravissimum Educationis* #4)

In other words, effective teaching facilitates the church's mission and apostolate unto the world.

> Catholic education is an expression of the mission entrusted by Jesus to the Church . . . Through education the Church prepares its members to proclaim the Good News and to translate this proclamation into action . . . Education is one of the most important ways by which the Church fulfills its commitment to . . . building the community (United States Conference of Catholic Bishops, *To Teach as Jesus Did* #'s 7 and 11, 1972)

Therefore, deacons must:

27

... with patience promote the liturgical instruction of the faithful and also their active participation ... taking into account their age, condition, way of life and standard of religious culture. (*Sacrosanctum Concilium* #27 and *Prebyterorum Ordninis* #5)

## Deacons and Ecclesial Tradition, Marriage and Holy Orders

As ministers of the word entrusted with preaching and with interpreting and teaching the word, deacons, likewise, serve to perpetuate the faith tradition by ensuring the ongoing intelligibility and viability of the faith. Therefore, diaconal ministry of the word is a service unto ecclesial tradition, i.e., a ministerial service of handing on the faith. The Second Vatican Council presented tradition as a living, growing, and developing reality, necessitating that the church perpetually discern how best to formulate doctrines of the faith as well as identify those formulations which are no longer useful.[5]

> Tradition ... makes progress in the Church with the help of the Holy Spirit. There is growth in insight into the realities and words that are being passed on. This comes about in various ways ... Thus, as centuries go by, the Church is always advancing towards the plenitude of divine truth ... (*Dei Verbum* #8)

As previously discussed, the Truths necessary for salvation (big-"T" Truths), which are perennially enduring in nature, are one thing ... the human formulation, articulation and communication (little-"t" truths) of these Truths are another. Rendering big-"T" Truths meaningful and relevant to humanity is the perennial law of evangelization and a fundamental mission of the church which has received its mandate from Jesus to go forth and share the gospel with all people. As preachers, teachers and illuminators of revelation and Scripture, deacons have an important role in this ecclesiological mission of perpetuating tradition. Indeed, given that

---

5. See Gaillardetz and Clifford, *Keys to the Council*, 41.

the majority of deacons are married, have families and hold secular employment, their life experiences frequently more readily resonate and are commonly more consistent with those of the majority of the lay faithful. A deacon's existential, historical and experiential realities often mirror and reflect the life experiences of the lay faithful whom they serve. Therefore, deacons have a significant ability to pass along the ecclesial tradition in a manner that speaks to and is applicable to the lived experience of the faithful.

In addition to their experiences as husbands, fathers and workers, deacons are also sacramentally visible ministers within the hierarchy of the church due to the sacrament of holy orders which they receive and whose ministry they put into praxis. Deacons receive the sacrament of holy orders and, therefore, an indelible ontological mark upon their soul whereby they are configured to Christ and empowered by the Spirit with a unique charism to act in the person of Christ the servant. Deacons are ordained *non ad sacerdotum, sed ad ministerium* (not unto the priesthood but unto a ministry of service—see *Lumen Gentium* #29). Deacons are ontologically conformed to Christ as an icon of service. Pope Paul VI spoke of deacons as being empowered by the Spirit with the unique gift of being the church's driving force of service. Diaconal service is typically described in terms of service to the church and world via ministries of sacrament, word and charity.

> ... deacons serve the People of God in the ministry of the liturgy, of the word, and of charity. (*Lumen Gentium* #29)

As an icon deacons serve to bridge the people with the transcendent (God and the bishop). As an icon the deacon's value and efficacy is not to be found in the deacon himself, nor his orders ... rather it is found in his ability to serve as an effective symbol which points to and makes present a reality other than himself (God, Jesus, bishop). True to the very nature of the sacrament, a deacon's efficacy is not to be found in themselves but in their ability to point beyond themselves via the quality of their lived witness. An additional charism bestowed by diaconal ordination is, therefore, a gift of the Spirit meant to aid the deacon in conforming himself to the humility of Christ.

The *sacra potestas* (sacred power) which ordination affords can be said to be expressed sacerdotally (priest) and *kenotically* (deacon). Ordained so as to be conformed to Jesus the servant, deacons exemplify and give witness to the paradoxical nature of ecclesial power. Although recipients of holy orders and members of the ecclesial hierarchy, a deacon's power is not one of authority via juridical governance and oversight, rather it is a *kenotic* (self-emptying, self-sacrificial love unto others) power which exemplifies and gives witness to the *kenotic* power of Jesus the servant who did not come to be served but to serve and to give his life as a ransom for many (see Matthew 20:28).

> Through ordination the deacon is empowered . . . with a kenotic power, a power or strength to empty himself in service to the church . . . those who would be leaders in the community of disciples are to be identified by their own self-sacrificing love in imitation of the kenosis of Christ . . . [6]

> The ministerial diaconate sacramentalizes the self-emptying love of Christ on behalf of others . . . through the sacramental grace received at ordination the deacon receives the strength to empty himself in the service of others . . . [7]

Additionally, for those who are married, deacons are also sacramentally graced towards *kenosis* via the sacramental grace of marriage and family life. Within the context of marriage and family life the married deacon exercises *kenotic* service via the offering of his will to his wife and via the self-emptying and self-sacrificial care and love he affords his children. In this way, marriage and family life both bestow upon the deacon additional sacramental grace (via the sacrament of marriage), i.e., additional help from God and the Holy Spirit to love and serve *kenotically*, and provide

---

6. Ditewig, "Charting a Theology of the Diaconate," 44–45.

7. Ditewig, *Emerging Diaconate*, 155.

the deacon with a context and community (family life) in micro-cosm which serves as a template for the macrocosmic ecclesial community he is ordained to serve. Indeed, traditionally marriage and family life have been defined sacramentally as symbols of God's love for humanity and Christ's love for the church—precisely what the Second Vatican Council called the church to be vis-à-vis the world when identifying the church to be missionary by nature and a servant and sacrament unto the world. Additionally, contemporary theology speaks of the family as the domestic church, school of social virtue and the primary and vital cell of society. Therefore, marriage and family not only afford the deacon additional sacramental grace unto *kenosis* but also provide a community in which the deacon exercises the type of *kenotic* service he is called to provide the wider ecclesial community via ordination/holy orders. That which is learned, experienced and lived within the context of marriage and family life is to be broadened out to the deacon's service to the wider church.

Vatican II describes marriage as a community of life and love which is an act of ecclesial worship and expression of faith that serves as a sign of the church's unity and witnesses to the presence of Christ. Furthermore, the council emphasizes marriage as a covenantal community of love—the sacrament is constituted by the mutual giving of self to the other exchanged by the spouses. This serves as a symbol of God's love for humanity and Christ's love for the church. This symbolic love is lived in the midst of the world and, hence, can draw others to know and experience the love of God. This is precisely the primary ecclesiological objective of Vatican II when the council defined the church to be a sacrament—and what a deacon is sacramentally called upon to do via holy orders. Hence, married life is a model and example of what the church and a deacon are to be to the world. Here we can see how married life is, indeed, the "domestic church."

> The family, because it arises from marriage, which is an image of the covenant of love of Christ and the church, and a participation in this covenant, will disclose to all the living presence of the savior in the world, as well as

show also the authentic nature of the church. (*Gaudium et Spes* #48)

Married persons, themselves . . . will bear witness, by their faithful love in the joys and sacrifices of their calling, to that mystery of love which the Lord revealed to the world by His death and resurrection. (*Gaudium et Spes* #52)

Emphasizing the importance of family life and Christian education Vatican II sees marriage as intimately linked to the wellbeing of society and the church.

The Apostolate of married persons and of families has a special importance for both the church and civil society. (*Apostolicam Actuositatem* #11)

The well-being of the individual person and of both human and Christian society is closely bound up with the healthy state of conjugal and family life. (*Gaudium et Spes* #47)

The church's social mission is one of striving to bring to realization the covenantal love between Christ and the church via social justice. Families can embody these ideals in their day to day life and activities, i.e., they can incarnate the ideals of love, reconciliation, justice, peace, hospitality, etc. In doing so, marriage, once again, serves as a model of what the church is to be to the world as well as a perennial school of the church's social teachings. Marriage and family life can serve as the building blocks of an ecclesiology which strives to bring to realization the church as sacrament, as well as a global order based upon peace and justice—this is the notion that Vatican II emphasizes in its situating of marriage within the context of the church's sacramental identity and social mission as evidenced in the dedication of an entire chapter to marriage in *Gaudium et Spes, The Pastoral Constitution on the Church in the Modern World*. In short, marriage is to prefigure the just society that the sacramental identity of the church is to help bring to realization.

The mission of being the primary vital cell of society has been given to the family by God Himself. This mission will be accomplished if the family . . . offers active hospitality and practices justice and other good works for the benefit of others . . . Christian families bear a very valuable witness to Christ before the world when all their life they remain attached to the Gospel and hold up the example of Christian marriage. (*Apostolicam Actuositatem* #11)

The family is the first school of those social virtues which every society needs . . . It is through the family that children are gradually introduced into civic partnership with their fellow human beings . . . (*Gravitisimus Educationis* #3)

Marriage serves to build up the kingdom of God in history by participating in the life, mission and sacramental identity of the church:

Husband and wife find their proper vocation in being witnesses to one another and to their children of faith in Christ and love for Him. The Christian family boldly proclaims both the present virtues of the Kingdom of God and the hope of a blessed life to come. Thus by its example and witness it . . . enlightens those who seek the truth. (*Lumen Gentium* #35)

Likewise, by having children and nurturing them the spouses communicate the nature of God's love to the world. Family life is intended to be an environment in which we can grow in all the unique dimensions of our individuality. Vatican II's appreciation for cultural pluralism and its emphasis on the innate dignity of each human being challenges the church to create a global environment in which the uniqueness of each individual can come to fruition. Hence, the family is absolutely indispensable for the realization of the church's social mission. Family teaches the skills needed to transform the world. It teaches us how to create communities for family life requires an ongoing willingness and effort to be present in a personal way to one another, and it demands a level of intimate sharing, caring and communicating, and the acceptance of the difficulties and sacrifices that this involves. Interdependence which exists between family members contributes to a better understanding of the responsibilities we have toward solidarity with others and the practice of subsidiarity—the very cornerstones of any efforts to achieve social justice. Through family we grow in our abilities to respect one another and learn to share in an equitable way. This, in turn, sensitizes us to injustices taking place within society. Via the love we receive from our family members we can discover that persons are gifts which communicate God's love to us—persons are sacraments! This inspires us to love others in return, thus perpetuating God's love for us all. The mutual and reciprocal exchange of love and forgiveness between family members serves as a sacrament of Christ's own *kenotic* love for us. In this way, married life contributes to Vatican II's ecclesial task to be a sacrament of Christ to the world.

Within the context of marriage and family life the deacon is called to *kenotically* serve others. The sacrament of marriage provides additional grace to the deacon to conform himself to the *kenosis* of Jesus the servant. Marriage and family life provides a forum for the deacon to live out and to teach Catholic Social Thought. Marriage and family life provide the deacon a setting in which the characteristics and principles that are to be marks of the church can be enacted, experienced and lived out. Marriage and family life call upon the deacon to create and establish a community of persons committed to the kingdom of God. As such, marriage and family life can inform a deacon's *kenotic* service to the wider ecclesial community and world. In short, marriage and family life are yet additional ways and means by which deacons are bearers of the church's sacramental, ministerial, ecclesiological and social justice traditions.

The indwelling of the Spirit afforded by ordination coupled with the deacon's unique context—marriage and family; employment; ministry—provide him with unique empathetic insights vis-à-vis family life, the secular world and the church's ministerial hierarchy. Hence the deacon is an effective bridge between these various vocations as well as an effective emissary of the bishop. Ordination and marriage afford the deacon a charism of availability whereby the Spirit aids him in externalizing the love of God and the work of the Spirit. As we have seen from our considerations of the history of the diaconate (see chapter 1), this role as bridge and emissary was prevalent in the early church. Much needs to be done in contemporary theological considerations of the diaconate to restore these roles/functions. Additionally, consideration of the Second Vatican Council's teachings regarding the episcopacy ought to inform theological considerations of the diaconate, particularly teachings regarding collaboration, cooperation, communion, solidarity, subsidiarity, consultation and the acknowledgement and empowerment of communal charisms—teachings operative and lived out within healthy marriages and families.

Historically orders had come to be defined vis-à-vis the presbyterate. Vatican II not only contextualized orders vis-à-vis baptism, but also sought to more clearly distinguish and differentiate the varying charisms associated with the three grades of orders: episcopate; presbyterate; diaconate. Via orders deacons are empowered by the Spirit to serve the church in sacrament, word and charity.

> Sacrament and Word—assist at liturgy; carry and proclaim the Gospel; preach; offer petitions and prayers; lead the penitential rite; call for the exchange of peace; prepare the altar and gifts; raise the cup; help distribute communion; return unused hosts to the tabernacle; offer the dismissal; take the Eucharist to the homebound, sick; facilitate benediction; commission apostolates; baptize; marry; conduct services for the deceased; offer marriage preparation; provide healing ministries.

Consequently, in preaching and catechesis, deacons must learn how to communicate the gospel effectively and integrally to persons in diverse stages of life and faith and who come from a myriad of diverse cultural experiences.

> Charity—teach and manifest the spiritual and corporal works of mercy and the principles of Catholic Social Teaching. (see *Lumen Gentium* #29)

As discussed above, these aspects of diaconal charity can be vitally shaped and informed by the sacrament of marriage. Therefore, in addition to the credibility which their life situations lend to their ministry, deacons also enjoy a stature of authority and esteem as recipients of the sacrament of holy orders and their place within the hierarchy of the church. Combined, these aspects and dimensions of the deacon lend to a unique credibility the deacon holds in the eyes of the faithful, thereby rendering them efficacious bearers of tradition.

Much still needs to be done to clarify and fortify the deacon's unique participation in the sacrament of holy orders so as to ensure the deacon's rightful stature as one ordained. Explanations which might tend to present deacons as sub-priests are not appropriate, adequate or sufficient. Nor are explanations which reduce deacons to merely functional agents. What is needed are renewed inquiries into diaconal participation in holy orders and a recovery of the historical intimacy deacons shared with bishops. A better understanding of the inter-relationship between the sacraments of marriage and diaconal orders is also needed. A renewed theological explanation of diaconal participation in holy orders (informed by marriage) coupled with a recovery of the deacon's relationship with the bishop will do much to enhance and fortify the deacon's place within the church's hierarchy and thereby edify the deacon's credibility.

As we saw in the previous chapter, the deacon historically served as the eyes, ears, mouth and hands of the bishop. Contemporary church teaching regarding the diaconate also accentuates the deacon's unique relationship to the bishop. Much needs to be done to put into contemporary ecclesial practice what this unique relationship between bishop and deacon might yield for the contemporary church. How might deacons be an extension of the bishop—as they were in previous centuries—in a manner that serves, builds up and edifies the contemporary church? How might contemporary deacons serve as mediators between the bishop and the faithful . . . presenting the needs of the faithful to bishops and the teachings of bishops to the faithful? Ought there be diocesan diaconal councils as there are diocesan presbyteral councils? Might deacons have a place on diocesan advisory boards and pastoral councils? Most dioceses have annual priestly convocations whereby the bishop engages the presbyterate . . . yet most lack a similar event for bishops and deacons to interact. In fact, in contemporary ecclesial practice there is very little engagement between bishop and deacons both prior to and subsequent to diaconal ordination. More needs to be done to evidence that:

> The deacon . . . is in direct relationship with the diocesan bishop . . . (United States Conference of Catholic Bishops, *National Directory* #41)

> The deacon is ordained to serve the ministry of episcope. In other words, the ministry of the deacon must be understood . . . by his public service to the apostolic ministry of episcope . . .[8]

Diaconal service is aimed towards the church's mission—of preaching the gospel, providing the sacraments and embodying the spiritual and corporal works of mercy (the stole which the deacon wears is a symbol of Christ the foot washer). This mission is universal in scope and extends from the deacon's ordination and relationship to the bishop. In the remaining chapters we will explore how diaconal service advances the mission of the church, empowers the laity in the living out of their baptismal dignity and contributes to the church's commitment to ecumenism and inter-religious dialogue, peace and the dignity of all persons.

---

8. Gaillardetz, "On the Theological Integrity of the Diaconate," 86–87.

# 3

# A Servant Church and
# Diaconal Ministry

## Deacons as Agents of Ecclesial
## Missiology and Service

THE SECOND VATICAN COUNCIL advanced an expanded notion
of mission into Roman Catholic thought. Prior to the twentieth
century, missionary activity was understood to be the activity of
a select few—namely white, male, foreign priests and mission-
orientated religious. Lay involvement in missionary activity was
infrequent and the church as a whole tended to be isolated from
missionary activity. Missionary activity tended to be understood
in territorial terms, i.e., lands identified and placed under the ju-
risdiction of the Congregation for the Propagation of Faith. Two
prevalent approaches tended to color Roman Catholic missiology:
1) the Munster School (Joseph Schmidlin), which was strongly
influenced by Protestant missiology, which chiefly emphasized the
proclamation of the gospel and the conversion and salvation of
all peoples; 2) a curial-canonist method (Pierre Charles), which
stressed the implantation of the church and the establishment of
the hierarchy, the foundation of indigenous churches and winning
over non-Catholics. Correspondingly a rather narrow assessment of missionary activity dominated, i.e., emphasis on visible

activities (quantity of baptisms and number of ecclesial buildings) at the expense of the spiritual and sociocultural dimensions (missionary activity has to do with the Spirit building up the Body of Christ and peoples, not just human undertakings).[1]

During the fifty years prior to the council, missions were gradually addressed:

- Benedict XV *Maximum Illud* 1919—renewed missionary energy was needed; do not confuse the gospel and nationalism

- Pius XI *Rerum Ecclesia* 1926—grow indigenous churches and local clergy

- Pius XII *Evangelii Praecones* 1951—mission involves the laity's renewal of the social order; indigenous cultures must be respected and preserved

- John XXIII *Princeps Pastorum* 1959—all the above (identifies Matteo Ricci as an exemplar).[2]

Missiology was beginning to recognize the need to be in dialogue with the world as missionary efforts were being affected by changes in technology, industrialization, politics and other social factors. Consequently, missiology would benefit greatly from the council's commitment to the modern world: "The Second Vatican Council . . . resolutely addresses . . . the whole of humanity . . . in the context of everything which envelopes them" (*Gaudium et Spes* #2).

The council fathers understood that the understanding of any/all Christian doctrines must enter into and correlate with human experience if they are to be experienced as meaningful and relevant. The council affirmed this with its silence regarding any specific missiological methods to be employed, and by proffering only universal guiding principles. It can be said that the transformation of cultures was a constitutive dimension of the council's understanding of missionary activity (see *Gaudium et Spes* #58 and *Ad Gentes Divinitus* #22). In short, development and humanization came to be seen as part of the church's missionary task, i.e., the

---

1. See Bevans, "Decree on the Church's Missionary Activity," 35f.
2. See Richard, "Vatican II and the Mission of the Church," 58f.

healing and elevating of human dignity; the fostering of solidarity; and the endowing of daily life with deeper meaning (see *Gaudium et Spes* #'s 40 and 42). "The mission of the Church is carried out by means of that activity through which . . . the Church makes itself fully present to all peoples . . ." (*Ad Gentes Divinitus* #5).

The council developed a Trinitarian model to explain missionary activity: missions originate from God's salvific plan; mission work is a continuation of Jesus' work; the Holy Spirit is present and active in such work (see *Ad Gentes Divinitus* #4). Therefore, the missionary apostolate came to be recognized as participating in the realization of the divine plan for human salvation (see *Ad Gentes* #7); assisting the renewal and progression of humanity (see *Ad Gentes* #8); and gathering the people of God into community in preparation for the Parousia (see *Ad Gentes* #9).

We human beings are subjects of history and as such we demand answers regarding appropriate conduct in the here now—questions and answers which emerge from our histories themselves. Consequently, we must avoid ecclesial dualisms which tend to suggest a disjoin between the church's concerns for the transcendent and temporal.

> It is a mistake to think that, because we have here no lasting city, but seek the city which is to come, we are entitled to shirk our earthly responsibilities . . . One of the gravest errors of our time is the dichotomy between the faith which many profess and the practice of their daily lives . . . Let there, then, be no such pernicious opposition between professional and social activity on the one hand and religious life on the other. The Christian who shirks their temporal duties shirks their duties toward their neighbor, neglects God himself, and endangers their eternal salvation. (*Gaudium et Spes* #43)

It is precisely in the historical that the church must evidence her transcendent dimension. To do this, theology must embrace a concrete, existential and historical point of view. In short, the church must see herself as being at the service of others (not herself). The *ad intra* life of the church ought to always lead her forth *ad extra* to those outside. The church's *ad intra* cultivations are, indeed, necessary, but when we press for her very purpose, her reason for existence, it is so that she may be sent into the world so as to continue to mediate God's revelation to the world, rendering it actual and available to others. The church has been founded so as to continue the work of Christ in the world. The church has been established for *diakonia*/service.

The church's missionary apostolate has two main foci: the world and the actualization of the church as a sacrament of Christ. These foci are made clear insofar as the church successfully manifests herself in history via her institutions, public functions, commitment of resources, the faithful's lived example, etc. Only if she is successful in her efforts to evidence herself in concrete, historical and existential terms will she be an effective sign of God's transcendence and its meaning for the world. The church's credibility as a sacrament depends upon her success in her historical manifestation and mediation (see *Ad Gentes Divinitus* #'s 16, 18, 22, 40).

Obviously, this understanding flows from the council's wider ecclesiological self-understanding which accentuated that the church, itself, is a sacrament (see *Gaudium et Spes* #'s 21, 42, 45). The vision of the church as sacrament provides the theological umbrella under which the church as missionary is defined (see *Ad Gentes Divinitus* #1). It also integrates the laity into the missiological process in more direct and meaningful ways. Mission work is presented as the responsibility of the whole church (see *Ad Gentes Divinitus* #'s 5, 28, 35 and *Gaudium et Spes* #'s 27, and 43), an activity facilitated via Christian witness (see *Ad Gentes Divinitus* #'s 11, 21, 35, 36, 41). As such, missionary activity is not to be seen as activity on the periphery of the church, but activity located at the very heart of her apostolate. Missionary activity is demanded by her own essential universality (see *Ad Gentes Divinitus* #1 and *Gaudium et Spes* #2). Only through mission work can the church realize herself as the universal sacrament of salvation. Consequently, "the Church is by its very nature missionary" (*Ad Gentes Divinitus* #2).

All Christians are to be missionaries if Vatican II's ecclesiological vision is to be realized and if the church is to be an efficacious sacrament of Christ unto the world. *Lumen Gentium* dedicates an entire chapter to the universal call to holiness in which all Christians are deemed to be disciples of Jesus and are called to an apostolate of Christian holiness vis-à-vis the world. Providing an example of holiness is not just a task for missionaries and clergy, but for all of the baptized. Via baptism all Christians are made sharers in Jesus' threefold dignity and ministries of priest, prophet and king (see *Lumen Gentium* #'s 31 and 33). This baptismal dignity bestows upon all Christians the responsibility to provide an *ad extra* witness of the faith unto the world. As sharers in Jesus' priestly ministry *ad extra*, all Christians are to live a life of holiness in the midst of the world (see *Lumen Gentium* #34). By sharing in Jesus' prophetic ministry *ad extra*, all of the baptized have the responsibility to provide a counter-cultural witness unto gospel values (see *Lumen Gentium* # 35). And via sharing in Jesus' kingly ministry *ad extra* all of the baptized have an obligation to infuse and impregnate the temporal realm with the spirit of the gospel via working for social justice (see *Lumen Gentium* #36 and *Apostolicam Actuositatem* #'s 2, 5, 7).[3] When the faithful live out their baptismal dignity they not only advance the church's missionary mandate, they also share in the church's role of advancing the redemptive designs of God for humanity (see *Lumen Gentium* #31).

> The lay apostolate is exercised when the laity work at the evangelization and sanctification of humanity; it is exercised, too, when they endeavor to have the Gospel Spirit permeate and improve the temporal order, going about it in a way that bears witness to Christ and helps forward the salvation of humanity. The characteristic of the lay state being a life in the midst of the world and of secular affairs, the laity are called by God to make of their apostolate, through the vigor of their Christian Spirit, a leaven in the world. (*Apostolicam Actuositatem* #7)

3. See Tkacik and McGonigle, *Pneumatic Correctives*, 19–26.

By reason of their special vocation it belongs to the laity to seek the kingdom of God by engaging in temporal affairs and directing them towards God's will. They live in the world ... There they are called by God ... to contribute to the sanctification of the world ... especially by the witness of their life ... (*Lumen Gentium* #31)

The laity are given a special vocation: to make the Church present and fruitful in those places and circumstances where it is only through them that she can become the salt of the earth. Thus, every lay person ... is at once the witness and living instrument of the mission of the Church itself. (*Lumen Gentium* #33)

The Church is not truly established and does not fully live, nor is a perfect sign of Christ unless there is a genuine laity existing and working alongside the hierarchy. For the Gospel cannot become deeply rooted in the mentality, life and work of people without the active presence of lay people. (*Ad Gentes* #21)

Given Vatican II's self-imposed ecclesial disposition of openness and its orientation of the church's apostolate *ad extra* to the world, it is easy, indeed, to the see how the hallmark of the church is to be *diakonia*/service. It only makes sense, therefore, that those within the church ordained for service and ontologically conformed to Jesus the servant, graced with the charism of service, and who are the church's service sacramentalized—deacons—ought to play a definitive role in bringing to realization Vatican II's vision of the church as missionary by nature. "Strengthened by sacramental grace deacons are dedicated to the People of God ... in service ... and works of charity" (*Lumen Gentium* #29).

The deacon's ministry of service is linked with the missionary dimension of the Church . . . The deacon is a specific sacramental sign . . . of Christ the servant . . . the deacon sacramentalizes the mission of the Church in his words and deeds. (United States Conference of Catholic Bishops, *National Directory* #'s 3, 37–38, 2005)

Such a connection between deacons and missionary service is consistent with the scriptural underpinning of the diaconate found in the Book of Acts which presents ministry marked by *diakonia* as one aimed at addressing the needs of *ad extra* communities drawn into the church's fold (e.g., Greek speaking converts discussed in Acts 6). It also resonates with a consistent role deacons served in the patristic era whereby they frequently acted as emissaries of bishops and were tasked with being the eyes, ears and mouth of the bishop, i.e., servants entrusted with learning the pastoral needs of faith communities and reporting these said needs back to the bishop. So, too, did the more immediate influences upon the council act as additional impetuses towards viewing the diaconate through a missiological lens, namely the German Caritas Movement, Second World War, horrors of the Shoah, and concerns of bishops in mission territories. Collectively these influences informed the council's re-establishment of the permanent diaconate so as to resurrect within the church an ordained ministry deemed requisite for the church to go forth into the world in a more formal, sacramental and effective manner so as to be more effective in addressing pastoral demands presented by the modern world.[4]

If deacons are to play such a definitive role in actualizing the council's missionary orientation, then they must embrace the missionary impulse of the church themselves:

> Diaconal service ought to be marked by leading, inspiring, enabling, and modeling for other members of the church what servant-leadership can mean in living the demands of Christian discipleship in the contemporary world . . . The deacon can make others aware of the connection between faith and life.[5]

Via their lives and their ministry, deacons are able to evidence, exemplify, and give witness to the church's missionary nature. Diaconal participation in holy orders calls deacons not only to ministry of sacrament and word (*ad intra*) but also to charity (*ad*

---

4. See Ditewig, *Emerging Diaconate*, 95–102.

5. Ditewig, "Charting a Theology of the Diaconate," 55–57.

*extra*). As part of their formation process deacons are assigned to an apostolate aimed at extending their *diakonia* beyond the church proper by having them serve in prisons, hospitals, assisted living centers, food pantries and soup kitchens, homeless shelters, etc. Such ministries are to mark their participation in orders and, therefore, should continue subsequent to ordination. By continuing such ministries deacons, indeed, lead and show by example what a constitutive aspect of Christian discipleship is, namely serving Jesus by serving those in need (see Matthew 25). Such a lived witness can do much to inspire others, and deacons can assume leadership roles in social ministries within parishes after ordination whereby they can promote, facilitate and enable others to become involved in such mission-orientated ministries. In short, deacons must also inspire and empower the laity to learn, understand, embrace and live out their missionary roles within the church's missionary apostolate. Via their ministries deacons are able to extend the church's missionary impulse among the lay faithful and out into the communities their parishes serve.

> . . . every way of being a deacon must be identifiable and recognizable as a form of service, inviting and empowering others to serve in such a way that communion with God and communion among people is advanced. That is pragmatically what it means to be church and what it means to be a deacon in the church.[6]

## The Church as Pilgrim and the Context of Diaconal Ministry

In addition to deeming the church to be missionary by nature, the Second Vatican Council also identified the church to be a pilgrim church, i.e., a community called by God, vivified by the Holy Spirit, and endowed with God's grace by which it derives its holiness, sojourning amongst all peoples toward an eschatological *telos*. As it sojourns among peoples, the church is to be a sacrament of Jesus inviting all persons to universal salvation which is willed by God

6. Cummings, "State of the Question," 28–29.

(see *Sacrosanctum Concilium* #5). As such, God is perpetually and perennially active within the church so as to lead all persons to himself (see *Lumen Gentium* #48). However, reciprocally, God also reveals himself to members of the church through the faces and lives of those with whom members come into contact. Hence, like a pilgrim, the church is edified by its journey and by those who bear vestiges of God thereby lending to experiences of intimacy with Jesus (see *Lumen Gentium* #50).

Deacons have a unique role to play within the pilgrim church and its dialectic of mutual enrichment between itself and the people which it encounters for deacons are ordained precisely unto a ministry of charity while also being existentially immersed within the *ad extra* temporal sphere through their work and the experiences of their marriages and family life. As the mission and ministries of the church unfold in the history and experiences of each and all persons as the church proleptically journeys towards its consummation with the realization of the kingdom of God, deacons are uniquely situated to give witness to the gospel lived in a variety of places for they live, work and exercise their ministries in a myriad of diverse settings.

The concept of church as pilgrim combines the historical existence of the church as it journeys through the various epochs of history, as well as the eschatological phenomena which awaits her (see *Lumen Gentium* #'s 48–49 and *Gaudium et Spes* #'s 39–40, 57). The eschatological dimension of this notion ought to energize our efforts in humanizing the world (see *Gaudium et Spes* #'s 21, 39 and 57), for culture bears positive values which can prepare persons for the gospel (see *Gaudiuem et Spes* #57). As we understand it, this vision of the church is one that is inspired by the Hebrew notions of peace, justice and righteousness, and the Christian vision of the reign of God which is to be marked by the absence of hunger and poverty, care for the ill and marginalized, liberation of the oppressed, and love. Consequently, the notion has much to do with the apostolate of social justice and the transformation of society and culture (see *Gaudium et Spes* #43). Again, Vatican II's orientation of the church and diaconate finds resonance with the scriptural description of diaconal ministries described in the New Testament and among numerous patristic sources which cite distribution of alms, ecclesial financial oversight, care of widows and orphans, visiting the sick, caring for the dying and dead, administering communal justice, etc. as ministries provided by deacons.

## Ecclesial Inculturation and Diaconal Ministry

The understanding of the church as pilgrim also markedly reveals the church's historical existence and need to inculturate itself. Inculturation is a dialectical encounter between the faith and culture, a two way exchange which involves affirmation, questioning or refusing, and new possibilities. The Second Vatican Council recognized a mutually enriching dialectic between culture and human realization: One comes to a true and full humanity only through culture (*Gaudium et Spes* #'s 53 and 31). The council lays two foundation stones for the church's thinking regarding culture: 1) culture is intimately connected with the dignity of persons; 2) culture is intimately linked with the call of freedom to become more fully human.

Culture is so important for it shapes who one is—both on the conscious and unconscious levels by providing language, social structures, first principles, patterns of behavior and beliefs. There is never a cultureless Christianity nor a faithless culture, hence no one expression of the faith ought to be absolutized, and there must be a recognition that God's saving presence and self-disclosure is already operative in every culture, even prior to when explicit Christianity makes itself present (see *Nostra Aetate* #'s 1 and 2).

Placing our faith in relationship with cultures is what enables our tradition to remain living and effective:

> There are many ties between the message of salvation and human culture. For God . . . has spoken according to the culture proper to each epoch. Likewise the Church, living in various circumstances in the course of time, has used the discoveries of different cultures so that in her preaching she might spread and explain the message of

> Christ to all nations, that she might examine it and more deeply understand it, that she might give it better expression . . . (*Gaudium et Spes* #58)

Furthermore, tradition carries within it the effects of history. Therefore, cultural pluralism has legitimacy and value for it enables the church to communicate the truth of the gospel to all persons throughout history: At all times the church carries the responsibility of reading the signs of the times and of interpreting them in light of the Gospel (*Gaudium et Spes* #'s 4 and 58). Additionally, differing cultural situations can bring different dimensions of the gospel into new light and life (see *Gaudium et Spes* #'s 44, 58 and 62).

> The experience of past ages, the progress of the sciences, and the treasures hidden in the various forms of human culture, by all of which the nature of man himself is more clearly revealed and new roads to truth are opened, these profit the Church, too. For, from the beginning of her history she has learned to express the message of Christ with the help of the ideas and terminology of various philosophers, and has tried to clarify it with their wisdom, too. Her purpose has been to adapt the Gospel to the grasp of all as well as to the needs of the learned . . . Indeed this accommodated preaching of the revealed word ought to remain the law of all evangelization. For thus the ability to express Christ's message in its own way is developed . . . and at the same time there is fostered a living exchange between the Church and the diverse cultures of people . . . so that revealed truth can always be more deeply penetrated, better understood and set forth. (*Gaudium et Spes* #44)

Implicit here is the understanding that the church is not wedded to any single culture (see *Gaudium et Spes* #58). The story and vision of the faith continues to unfold throughout history and the faith remains a living tradition via becoming a current event in new times and places (see *Gaudium et Spes* #44). The church's catholicity rests upon the conviction that the truths and values of the faith can be appropriated by diverse cultures, and according to the mode of the receiver, while maintaining unity in faith. The values of God's reign ought to be evidenced in the very process of inculturation. The process of inculturation provides the church with a greater awareness of: the dignity of human persons; the presence and activity of the Holy Spirit; the dialectical process of evangelization; new ways to convey its message of the gospel; the social nature of faith; the mystery of the Incarnation (the pre-existent and co-eternal Logos entered into human culture thereby illuminating it while also being a product of it); and the mystery of redemption as the church embraces human realities so as to purify dehumanizing aspects of them.

As clergy who live and exercise their ministries both within the *ad intra* life of the church as well as in the midst of the cultural contexts in which they live, work and serve, deacons are well-suited to discerning ways and means of expressing the faith in a manner meaningful, relevant and viable to their particular cultural context.

> By being visibly at home in both the Church and the world the deacon embodies the great message of Vatican II, namely that the whole world is taken up in what happens at the altar and that the sacrifice of the altar is celebrated for the sanctification of the whole world.[7]

Deacons are also well positioned to listen to and learn from the diverse and pluralistic experiences of the people in the wide range of cultural settings in which they live, work and serve.

> Deacons should be able to evaluate their society and culture in light of the Gospel and to understand the Gospel in the light of the particular features of the society and culture in which he will be serving. (United States Conference of Catholic Bishops, *National Directory* #121, 2005)

Via critical reflection upon these diverse experiences, deacons can serve as pastoral agents helping the church to discover new ways and means of conveying the Christian message in manners that are appropriate and which complement the good inherent in these

---

7. McPartlan, "Deacon and *Gaudium et Spes*," 67.

diverse cultural settings (see *Lumen Gentium* #13; *Gaudium et Spes* #58; *Ad Gentes* #'s 19, 22).

> . . . the deacon should be conversant with contemporary cultures and with the aspirations and problems of his times . . . indeed, he is called to . . . assume the Church's responsibility of reading the signs of the times and interpreting them in light of the Gospel. (Congregation for the Clergy, *Directorium Pro Ministerio* #43, 1998)

In short, the Second Vatican Council committed the church to reaching people where they are and deacons are uniquely positioned to facilitate this said ecclesial aim.

As husbands, married deacons understand the cultural factors which impact and shape married life. They have firsthand experience of the demands associated with marriage and the cultural pressures and influences which pose challenges to a healthy marriage. They are also more likely to be in tune with the shifting cultural mores and ethos which are redefining our understanding and experiences of traditional and conventional relationships. Such firsthand/lived experiences can inform and edify deacons' roles in marriage counseling and preparation. Those deacons who are fathers will, likewise, have firsthand experience raising youth. As a parent such deacons will be exposed to contemporary cultural trends in social media, music, movies, technology, communication, preferred activities of the youth, dating habits of young adults, etc. as they raise their children. Correspondingly, they will have an understanding of how these trends impact our youth—positively and negatively. Such experiences can inform and edify deacons' roles in youth and young adult ministries.

The majority of permanent deacons are not only married but also are employed in work outside of their ecclesial duties. Therefore they will also have firsthand experience which comes with the demands of balancing work and family, work and faith life. Economic realities and working conditions operative within society will be well known to them, as will the challenges and stresses which come with work and trying to provide a secure lifestyle for their family and their children's futures. A right to work and a just wage and the right to associate, as well as a right to rest and leisure, are constitutive aspects of Catholic Social Thought as well as pressing issues in our contemporary society. The Magisterium has consistently championed marriage and family life and the priority of the subjective aspect of work (the worker over capital) over the past fifty years. In light of the aforesaid, deacons have firsthand experiences which enable them to be credible voices and advocates of these seminal teachings of the church.

Given their unique roles as husbands, fathers, workers and members of the church's ordained hierarchy, deacons can do much to advance the task of ecclesial inculturation and do so in a manner that is informed by the myriad of vantage points and perspectives which are derived from their various vocations. Such cosmopolitan vocational experiences enable deacons to draw lessons from their cultural experiences as well as from their theological training and sacramental character afforded by holy orders. Such a breadth of experience vis-à-vis the church-cultural dialectic positions the deacon well to help in the efforts to navigate between the extremes of rigid ecclesial dogmatism and licentious cultural relativism. In helping the church preserve the balance between these extremes, deacons are able to advance the Second Vatican Council's openness to inculturation in a manner that is respective of the goods that culture can offer and the wisdom articulated in the Magisterial teachings of the church. Doing so acknowledges and is faithful to the council's call to *aggiornamento* and to read the signs of the times. It also helps to ensure that the church continues to discover new ways and means of communicating (little-"t" truths) the Truths of the faith in a manner that is intelligible, meaningful and viable to contemporary persons. Doing so helps to ensure that the faith remains alive and relevant while acknowledging the caution voiced by the late saint and pope, John Paul II: "A faith that places itself on the margin . . . of culture . . . would be a faith unfaithful to the fullness of what the Word of God manifests and reveals, a decapitated faith, worse still, a faith in the process of self-annihilation" (Pope John Paul II, *Ex Corde Ecclesia* #44, 1990).

# 4

# The Church as Sacrament
# and Diaconal Ministry

## The Ecclesiology of the Second Vatican Council
## and Sacramental Reform

As we have seen in earlier chapters, the Second Vatican Council's ecclesiological emphasis on the church as servant and defining of the church's very essence and nature as being missionary informed yet another seminal ecclesiological positing of the council, namely that the church is herself a sacrament (see *Gaudium et Spes* #'s 21, 42, 45; *Lumen Gentium* #'s 1, 48 *Sacrosanctum Concilium* #26; and *Ad Gentes* #5).

> Since the Church is in Christ like a sacrament . . . it desires now to unfold more fully to the faithful of the Church and to the whole world its own inner nature and universal mission. (*Lumen Gentium* # 1)

As such, the church is to point to and make present Christ to the world.

> . . . the Church's mission is being a sacrament—a sign and instrument—manifesting and actualizing the mystery of God's love for humanity . . . and unity among all people. (*Gaudium et Spes* #'s 42 and 45)

"The church is the visible expression of Christ's grace realized in the form of a society which is a sign."[1] The church is the means by which Christ is perpetually given body so as to serve as a visible manifestation of God's saving activity.

> During the time of Christ's material absence, between His Ascension and His Parousia, the role of the sacraments, and the entire church and its apostolate is to extend to all the benefit of the Incarnation and the promise of the Resurrection, so as to invite all to Him . . . it is the means by which the historical coming of God for our salvation exists forever in the world.[2]

The church's sacramental identity can be said to have two dimensions: 1) vertical—intimate union with God; and 2) horizontal—the unity and peace of the whole human race (see *Apostolicam Actuositatem* #5; *Lumen Gentium* #36; and *Gaudium et Spes* #40). The two dimensions are always connected, suggesting that as part of the church's task in sharing the redemption of Jesus are actions for justice and peace for such actions enable us to be collaborators in Christ's redemptive work. In the years since the council this understanding of the church's role in the process of Christ's redemption being intricately connected to the liberation of peoples from all that oppress them has become consistently accentuated.

How does the church do this? How is the church to be a sacrament to the world? The church is to be an instrument which mediates grace via being a community whose life bears witness of God's love for humanity and Jesus' love for the church. The church must be a sign which is efficacious by rendering the past saving activity of Christ in the present with a view to a different future for the world.

> The Church becomes church insofar as the grace of Christ, operative within it, achieves historical tangibility through the actions of the Church . . . As believers succeed in finding appropriate external forms by which to express their commitment to God in Christ, they

1. Schillebeeckx, *Christ the Sacrament of Encounter with God*, 48.
2. Congar, *I Believe in the Holy Spirit*, 47–48.

become living symbols of divine love and beacons of hope in the world.[3]

Hence we must be forever mindful that visible/symbolic expressions of grace are perennially challenged to become more effective signs of Christ.

The church must also be a herald of the gospel so that narrative and values conveyed therein can shape the character of the faithful. The communal narrative of the church—the gospel—is a story which has the power to color the vision of the faithful. How the faithful see things, in turn, expands their imaginations, enabling them to construct a world view consistent with the message of Jesus. Such a world view informs the choices, attitudes, convictions and dispositions of the faithful. In short, assimilation of the gospel narrative heralded by the church shapes the character of the faithful. If one makes the values of the gospel one's own, these values predispose us to live a certain way. Character becomes a matter of making decisions based upon beliefs that one lives by and acting according to habits we have assimilated. Character is a social phenomena, formed as we internalize the narratives and the beliefs, values and loyalties conveyed within the communities to which we belong. Hence character is formed by our relationships and commitments.[4] The church needs to be a community in which the values of the gospel are perpetually and perennially proclaimed in a manner that enables the faithful to assimilate the values into their lives in ways and means that shape their character and that prove to be meaningful, relevant and life-giving. When the community which is church tells the stories of Jesus and embodies them in sacramental ritual and social action, Jesus is made present so that others may encounter him and commit themselves to him. The church makes discipleship a possibility. Discipleship equals Christian character. When we direct our freedom and loyalty to the person and message of Jesus we accept Jesus as the model of our actions and as the model

3. Dulles, *Models of the Church*, 64–67.

4. See Hanigan, *As I Have Loved You*, 25–100; and Gula, *Reasoned Informed by Faith*, 136–46, 185–219.

of the type of person that we are trying to become, i.e., we make Jesus the norm of our life and allow the Gospels to influence our: perspective; disposition, intentions, affections and praxis.[5] The church, or ecclesial community, is indispensable to discipleship for it is where the Christian narrative/story is proclaimed and it is where we are put in touch with Christian symbols via the sacraments. Hence, the church's influence on persons largely depends on how well the stories of faith are told and how well the rituals are structured and performed. If the church is to be a viable community then she must tell the stories of Jesus and embody them in her sacramental rituals and social actions in such a way that Christ is made present to others in a living and effective manner, i.e., the church must make an encounter with Jesus possible if persons are to embrace discipleship. The church's function, then, can be described as: transmitting (Jesus') values; providing tradition; shaping the identity of the faithful; integrating competing value claims; teaching skills; and providing a mission.[6] The church's success in these functions is intricately linked with the success of her symbols to: illuminate life's ambiguities; express the ultimate meaning and value of life; form attitudes and convictions; structure a way of life for the faithful.[7] The church's rituals (ceremonial observances or formal, solemn acts or procedures carried out in accordance with prescribed rules or customs) which embody and express her symbols socially must also be effective.[8]

## Diaconal Ministry:
## Sacramental Presidency and Assistance

Deacons, therefore, have a vital role ensuring the sacramental efficacy of the church and the shaping of the faithful's character for they have a privileged role in the church's sacramental economy

---

5. See Hanigan, *As I Have Loved You*, 25–100; and Gula, *Reasoned Informed by Faith*, 136–45; 185–219.

6. Hanigan, *As I Have Loved You*, 25–38.

7. Ibid., 78–87.

8. Ibid., 93.

for, as we have seen in chapter 2, they are ordained unto word and sacrament. As such, deacons are charismatically empowered with a formal and public office within the church whereby they are entrusted with communicating the Christian narrative via their proclamation of the gospel and their preaching. As voices of said narrative, deacons are heralds of the values inherent to the gospel. Via their proclamation and preaching, deacons render the gospel values intelligible, meaningful, relevant, viable and life-giving to those whom they minister, thereby playing a role in the formation of the characters of the faithful. Additionally, as ones afforded the ontological transformation and graces afforded by holy orders, deacons are also entrusted with roles of sacramental presidency. In their presiding roles within the church's sacramental economy, deacons, therefore, are in a position to illuminate and explicate the rich and deep meanings inherent within and conveyed by the symbols and rituals of the church's sacramental life. If deacons do so in manners and ways readily understood and assimilated by the faithful, they, again, play a pivotal role shaping and forming the attitudes, convictions and character of the faithful.

Additionally, the church ensures its efficacy as a sacrament by preserving the word and the apostolic faith. The fellowship of the church continues the teaching and witness of the apostles and acts as the venue through which the Word comes forth to unite human beings with himself. Furthermore, when the Word comes through the church, the Holy Spirit also comes, showing to all the gifts of the incarnate Christ, and creating faith in its hearers. Via the sacraments, too, does the church evidence its own sacramentality. Baptism affords one integration into the body of Christ and the Eucharist enables one to receive Jesus' body and blood and to be drawn into communion with him. Penance offers us the reconciling grace afforded to us as the result of Jesus' salvific Passion. Confirmation empowers us to proffer public witness on Jesus' behalf, as he did in his incarnate body and via his earthly ministry. Marriage is a perennial communion mirroring God's steadfast covenantal love for humanity and which renders Jesus present by giving witness to his *kenotic* offering of his will.

Anointing links us to the redemptive suffering of Jesus. Holy orders serves as an instrument of God's mediated service to others, as did Jesus via the Incarnation.

As previously noted, ordained unto sacramental service, deacons have an important role to play in this sacramental economy. Deacons can baptize and, therefore, ought to preside in a manner that communicates to the faithful the breadth and riches of the grace afforded by the sacrament, i.e., the remission of sin and rebirth into the life of Jesus; incorporation into the church, the body of Christ; the sharing of Jesus' threefold ministry as priest, prophet and king (see below). Deacons assist at the Eucharist via, as we have seen, their proclamation of the gospel and homiletical preaching. They also assist the priest in preparing the altar for the consecration of the bread and wine and bear the chalice of the precious blood before the gathered assembly. Deacons give witness to the power and grace of reconciliation via the myriad of interpersonal relationships their breadth of life experiences bespeaks. They are also frequently leaders of and/or are involved in ecclesial ministries which bespeak of God's forgiveness and reconciliation, e.g., prison ministry. The diaconate, itself, like confirmation, is a sacramental reality which enables deacons to assume a formal public role within the church aimed at building up the church and extending God's kingdom. As considered in chapter 2, married deacons are positioned within the church to evidence God's love for humanity and Christ's love for the church via their lived example as husband and father. Deacons are also able to preside at weddings and can draw upon their own lived experiences in the instruction, preparation and marrying of the faithful. Deacons are able to preside over funeral services and burials. In said roles they are able to comfort the faithful and afford them hope by illuminating the redemptive nature of suffering as evidenced by Jesus' Passion as well as the paradoxical nature of death which was transformed by the resurrection of Jesus. All of the aforesaid the deacon does as one who has received holy orders and is thereby ontologically and pneumatically empowered to serve as a mediating instrument of God's grace in a public and formal manner within the church as a member of the church's clergy/hierarchy.

Via discipleship and apostolates we are called to live out our faith in our very vocations, spreading into the world the example of our faith and the message/example of Christ. The apostolates are means by which we give body to and extend the Incarnation. Therefore discipleship and apostolates facilitate the efficacy of the church as sacrament as well. As the council identifies us, we are to be the people of God, i.e., *theophers* and *christophers*—bearers of God and Christ.

> The faith of the Christian life ought . . . to be manifested in the very midst of the world, within the Christian community and within daily life. Hence the Christian's task is to live out the calling of faith in terms of one's secular calling. That is the way we die unto the world. The value of the secular calling for Christians is that it provides an opportunity of living the Christian life . . . and engaging more vigorously in the conversion of the world . . .[9]

Hence the faithful utilize the things of the world, but use them for different purposes, i.e., as means to express and live out their faith in Christ. As such, their secular expressions serve to reveal Christ to others. In being sacraments themselves—via living out their lives in such a way that they point to and make Christ present—they facilitate the church's efforts at being a sacrament. The faithful's contribution to the church's effort to be a sacrament is particularly advanced in this regard when the faithful practice social justice, affirm the sacramentality of other human beings via deeming them to be the *imago dei,* promote solidarity and the common good, advocate economic justice and a preferential option for the poor, honor the principle of subsidiarity, practice stewardship and ardently work for peace. In sum, the principles of Catholic Social Teaching are key ways in which the faithful can bear witness unto gospel values within the secular realm and by doing so advance the church's sacramental identity. Christian discipleship is a matter of praxis, i.e., love and service in action! It can be said that every Christian

9. Bonhoeffer, *Cost of Discipleship,* 265.

is to be a sacrament, i.e., a sign/symbol which communicates and makes present God's love and grace upon those who receive them. Hence the Christian life places an awesome responsibility on its adherents to conduct themselves publicly in such a manner as to give witness to this love of God.

Diaconal ministry ought to be marked by efforts to assist the faithful in viewing themselves in light of the aforesaid. Deacons ought to inform the laity of their baptismal dignity and empower them to live it out (see below). When deacons do so, particularly the *ad extra* aspects, dimensions and expressions of one's baptismal dignity, they are, in turn, empowering the apostolates of the lay faithful, thereby enabling the laity to be the sacraments unto others/the world that they are meant to be. Diaconal ministry is a ministry that ought to advance the social justice apostolates of the laity. Again, as considered in chapter 2, deacons, as teachers and bearers of ecclesial tradition, ought to teach Catholic Social Thought and exemplify it in action, and commit themselves to ministries which help the laity to live in a manner that such teachings are put into praxis. In short, diaconal ministry ought not be divorced from the social apostolates of the laity, rather diaconal ministry ought to serve as a sign, icon, sacrament, driving force/ animus, sustainer and nourisher of said apostolates.

Vatican II took additional innovative steps to ensure that the church would serve as a sacrament of Christ to the world, including defining the church as a mystery and as the people of God. As mystery, the church is a community utilized by God in his providential designs for human salvation; founded by Jesus; and animated, vivified and sustained by the ongoing presence of the Holy Spirit (see *Lumen Gentium* ch. 1). As people of God the church is to be an instrument through which Christ brings to realization the kingdom of God. Hence the faithful have an obligation to extend the kingdom throughout the world via giving witness to all whom they meet. The church has received this obligation as a command from Christ, himself, and each and every member has been afforded charisms from the Spirit so as to play their part in this effort (see *Lumen Gentium* #'s 9, 10, 13, 17; *Ad Gentes* #5; and *Gaudium et*

*Spes* #40). Like the chosen people of God—the Jews—the church, too, is to be a sign unto the nations of God's love for humanity. As we have seen in prior chapters, Vatican II also defined the church's very nature to be missionary and asserted that the church's activity is to be the epiphany and manifestation of God's plan to the world (see *Ad Gentes* #'s 2, 9.) Additionally, to ensure its success in being an efficacious sacrament of Jesus unto the world the council also esteemed the role of the laity. Again, as previously considered, if the church is to be successful in being a sacrament of Christ to/ for the world then she must present herself to human beings in the situation in which they find themselves. Hence the Christian witness via example is indispensable to the church's sacramental nature. The very apostolate, or vocation, of the laity is the building up of the church in the world and the renewal of the temporal order. To the extent that the laity are faithful to their apostolate they serve to advance the church's salvific ministry (see *Ad Gentes* #'s 11, 12, 21, 36, *Gaudium et Spes* #43, *Lumen Gentium* #'s 31, 33; and *Apostolicam Actuositatem* #'s 1, 2, 5, 7). In later chapters we will consider how the council's advocacy of ecumenism, interreligious dialogue and peace, and championing of human dignity also lend to her efforts to be a sacrament.

If the laity are to be empowered to live as Christian witnesses within the world and thereby render the church a sacrament, then they need God's help, for the world is frequently indifferent and/or hostile to the values of the gospel. Grace is God's help. The sacraments communicate grace. Therefore, to ensure that the laity receive the grace needed to animate, nourish and sustain their apostolate in the world which the sacraments afford, the Second Vatican Council took prolific steps to reform the sacramental economy of the church. Indeed, the first document promulgated by the council was the *Decree on the Liturgy, Sacrosanctum Concilium*, dedicated to reforming the sacraments so as to ensure, above all else, the full conscious and active participation of the laity:

> In the restoration and promotion of the sacred liturgy
> the full and active participation by all the people is the
> aim to be considered before all else, for it is the primary

and indispensable source from which the faithful are to derive the true Christian spirit. (*Sacrosanctum Concilium* #'s 14 and 48)

If the ecclesiological vision of the council—which accentuated the church as servant, pilgrim, people of God, missionary by nature and sacrament—was to be realized, then the laity would need the grace of the sacraments to animate, nourish and sustain them and their efforts of living the gospel in the midst of the world. Therefore, the council sought to revise the sacraments so as to ensure that the laity understood what they were encountering in the church's sacramental life. Vatican II's reform of the sacraments was directed toward ensuring their ongoing meaning and relevance in the lives of the faithful:

> The Council also desires that, where necessary, the rites be revised carefully in the light of sound tradition, and that they be given new vigor to meet the circumstances and needs of modern times. (*Sacrosanctum Concilium* #4)

> . . . rites should be distinguished by a noble simplicity. They should be short, clear and free from useless repetitions. They should be within the people's powers of comprehension . . . (*Sacrosanctum Concilium* #34)

The council's reform of the sacraments was paramount to recovering the social and communal nature of the sacraments which was characteristic of the sacramental practices of the early church. To be such, the laity needed to have greater participatory roles within the sacramental economy:

> Liturgical services are not private functions but are celebrations of the Church . . . Therefore, liturgical services pertain to the whole Body of the Church. They manifest it and have effects upon it. (*Sacrosanctum Concilium* #26)

> . . . rites are meant to be celebrated in common, with the faithful present and actively participating . . . rather than by an individual or quasi privately. (*Sacrosanctum Concilium* #27)

> The Church, therefore, earnestly desires that Christ's
> faithful, when at this mystery of faith, should not be
> there as strangers or silent spectators; on the contrary,
> through a good understanding of the rites and prayers
> they should take part in the sacred action conscious of
> what they are doing, with devotion and full collabora-
> tion. (*Sacrosanctum Concilium* #48)

Greater participation of the laity in the church's sacramental life
was deemed by the council to be a right and duty of the laity by
virtue of them sharing in the *ad intra* priestly dignity of Jesus via
their baptism.

> Mother Church earnestly desires that all the faithful
> should be led to that full, conscious and active partici-
> pation in liturgical celebrations which is demanded by
> the very nature of the liturgy and to which the Christian
> people, "a chosen race, a royal priesthood, a holy nation,
> a redeemed people" (I Peter 2:9; 4–5) have a right and
> obligation by reason of their baptism. (*Sacrosanctum
> Concilum* #'s 14 and 27)

In addition to simplifying and rendering the sacraments more
intelligible to the laity, and to increasing the laity's participation in
the sacraments, the council also called for sacramental inculturation. The sacramental life of the church was to integrate various
aspects and dimensions drawn from the indigenous experiences of
the faithful which furthered the laity's understanding of and comfort within the church's sacramental life. Central to sacramental
inculturation was a call for more widespread use of the vernacular
in sacramental celebrations (see *Sacrosanctum Concilium* #'s 36
and 54). Additionally, art and music common to the people were
to be integrated into worship (see *Sacrosanctum Concilium* #'s
112, 118, 119 and 123). Even the architectural designs of churches
and the furnishings therein were to be reflective of the cultures of
peoples and aimed at inviting lay participation (see *Sacrosanctum
Concilium* #'s 122–24 and 128). Indeed, throughout the *Decree on
the Liturgy* reform of the sacraments unto greater lay participation
via liturgical inculturation is called for with the council entrusting

indigenous bishops, episcopal conferences and liturgical commissions with the facilitation and oversight of said efforts.

The reform of the sacraments was so important to the council fathers for the sacraments are the instruments through which the grace of God which animates, nourishes and sustains the lay apostolate (see *Lumen Gentium* #33). It is, in turn, the lay apostolate which ensures the efficacy of the church being an efficacious missionary servant and sacrament to the world. If Vatican II's making of a servant church is to be actualized, then the sacraments must be conducted in a manner which ensures that the laity encounter the grace of God in meaningful, relevant and life-giving ways. Deacons, as members of the clergy ordained unto sacrament, as well as word and charity, therefore, have a vital role to play in ensuring that the vision of church as missionary servant is brought to realization for, as previously noted, via orders they have the privileged responsibility of presiding over and/or assisting in sacramental celebrations.

> . . . deacons serve the People of God in the ministry of the liturgy, of the word, and of charity. (*Lumen Gentium* #29)
>
> It pertains to the office of a deacon . . . to administer Baptism . . . to be the custodian and distributor of the Eucharist . . . to assist and bless marriages, to bring Viaticum to the dying, to read the sacred Scripture to the faithful, to administer sacramentals, and to officiate at funeral and burial services. (*Lumen Gentium* #29)

It is crucially important that deacons conduct their sacramental presidency in a manner that keeps the primary objective and aim of Vatican II's sacramental reforms in mind—they must conduct their sacramental ministries with the experience of the laity foremost in thought and praxis. Deacons need to ensure that the laity are actively involved in the sacraments, understanding what their participation and roles entail. Deacons need to be sensitive to the cultural lived experiences of the faithful with whom they are celebrating and incorporate meaningful and relevant aspects from these cultural experiences into their presidency and proclamations.

Sacramental ministry and preaching offer a scriptural interpretation of human existence which enables the community to recognize God's active presence, to respond to that presence in faith through liturgical word and gesture, and beyond the liturgical assembly, through a life lived in conformity with the Gospel. (United States Conference of Catholic Bishops, *Fulfilled in Your Hearing* #29, 1982)

## Deacons: Empowering the Laity's Threefold Baptismal Dignity

Central to diaconal sacramental ministry is the empowering of the laity's baptismal dignity by which the Lord himself makes them sharers in the threefold ministries of Jesus as priest, prophet and king, and by which he appoints them to the apostolate.

> . . . the faithful who by baptism are incorporated into Christ are placed in the People of God and in their own way share the priestly, prophetic and kingly office of Christ . . . (*Lumen Gentium* #31)

The laity's baptismal dignity, in turn, informs and is the foundational basis from which their wider participation in the church's *ad intra* sacramental economy and *ad extra* apostolate of justice flow.

> The apostolate of the laity is a sharing in the salvific mission of the church. Through baptism and confirmation all are appointed to the apostolate by the Lord himself. (*Lumen Gentium* #33)

Hence, the privilege that deacons have via orders to baptize the faithful is an awesome responsibility. Deacons need to exercise their baptismal ministry in a manner that conveys this profound dignity associated with baptism, and in a manner that sows the seeds for the sacrament's eventual blooming as the baptized live out their threefold baptismal dignity within the life of the church and the world.

We associate one's priestly daptismal dignity *ad intra* with greater participation of the laity in the church's sacramental life. The Second Vatican Council's reform of the sacramental economy of the church, as noted above, explicitly called for such for the full, conscious and active participation of the laity is necessary for the full effects of the sacraments to be realized (see *Sacrosanctum Concilium* #'s 11 and 14). This is why the council called for attention to be given to the indigenous languages of the people (see *Sacrosanctum Concilium* #'s 36 and 54); the sacraments being adapted to the culture of the people (see *Sacrosanctum Concilium* #'s 37–40); availing Scripture a more prominent role in sacramental celebrations (see *Sacrosanctum Concilium* #'s 33 and 35); and the restoration of the homily and the general intercessions (see *Sacrosanctum Concilium* #'s 52–53). Furthermore, the council affirmed that the laity co-offer the Eucharist together with the priest (see *Lumen Gentium* #10 and *Eucharisticum Mysterium* #12); and contribute to the real presence of Jesus in the sacraments via their prayers, songs and gathered assembly (see *Sacrosanctum Concilium* #7). Also, the council linked the sacraments with the lay apostolate (see *Lumen Gentium* #33, *Sacrosanctum Concilium* #2 and *Actuositatem Apostolicam* #10).

Such unprecedented accentuation and affirmation of the laity's roles within the church's *ad intra* sacramental life warrants that deacons utilize their sacramental ministries in ways that make the laity's aforesaid importance within the sacramental economy known, embraced and lived.

We associate one's priestly baptismal dignity *ad extra* with the laity participating in the universal call to holiness within the midst of the world (see chapter 3 above and *Lumen Gentium's* chapter 5).

Vatican II associates the faithful's prophetic baptismal dignity *ad intra* with the laity being a part of the *sensus fidelium*:

> The holy People of God share also in Christ's prophetic office . . . The whole body of the faithful who have an anointing that comes from the holy one cannot err in matters of belief. This characteristic is shown in the

supernatural appreciation of the faith (sensus fidei) of
the whole people ... (*Lumen Gentium* #'s 12 and 35)

As considered in chapter 1, the historical role of deacons was
one marked by deacons serving as a mediator between bishops
and the laity. As successors to the apostles, bishops serve as the authoritative teachers and preservers of the authentic apostolic faith.
However, as was seen in chapter 1 and the Appendix, Vatican II
called for bishops to exercise their Magisterial teaching authority
in a manner that was consultative and respectful of the *sensus fidelium*, i.e., characterized by dialogue, collaboration, subsidiarity,
mutual recognition of charismatic gifts and professional competencies. If the council's teaching regarding the *ad intra* prophetic
baptismal dignity of the laity is to be properly acknowledged and if
the laity's Magisterial role as the *sensus fidelium* is to be respected,
then greater dialogue and collaboration between bishops and the
laity must occur and formalized ecclesial vehicles and instruments
which effect shared decision-making between bishops and the
faithful within the church must be developed and implemented.
Given the historical roles that deacons have served as mediators
between bishops and laity, and their roles as episcopal represen-
tatives, emissaries and envoys to regional conferences/synods, it
seems prudent to develop such ecclesial mechanisms, structures,
instruments and vehicles within the contemporary church with an
eye toward how deacons might be at the heart of and play a vital
role in the aforesaid. As we have seen, as clergy within the church
who have a place within the church's hierarchy as well as clergy
whose lives are most consistent and resonate with the lives of the
laity (frequently mirroring the lives of the laity in their marriages
and family life and their professional vocations), deacons are
uniquely positioned and sacramentally empowered to do so. Although demanding a kind of episcopal *kenosis* in matters pertinent
to ecclesial decision-making and teaching authority, developing
such a model of ecclesial teaching would do much to acknowledge
the breadth of the Spirit's gifts operative within the church, affirm
the *ad intra* prophetic dignity of the laity, recover an intrinsic mark
of the historical diaconate in a manner that bears new relevance

to the contemporary church, lend to the teaching credibility of bishops/the church, and advance the making of a servant church. The future development of such a model of ecclesial teaching holds yet untapped potential for the restored diaconate in the life of the contemporary church, yet is consistent with ecclesial tradition, history and precedent.

The prophetic baptismal dignity *ad extra* of the laity is exercised when they proffer a counter-cultural witness unto the values of the gospel (see chapter 3).

> They exercise the apostolate in fact by their activity directed to the evangelization and sanctification of men and to the penetrating and perfecting of the temporal order through the spirit of the Gospel. In this way, their temporal activity openly bears witness to Christ . . . Since the laity . . . live in the midst of the world and its concerns, they are called by God to exercise their apostolate in the world like leaven, with the ardor of the spirit of Christ. (*Apostolicam Actuositatem* #2)

We associate the kingly baptismal dignity *ad extra* with the laity exercising the apostolate of justice in the midst of the world (see above and previous chapters).

> Laymen ought to take on themselves as their distinctive task the renewal of the temporal order . . . Among the tasks of the lay apostolate Christian social action is preeminent. (*Apostolicam Actuositatem* #7)

> . . . they are assigned to the apostolate by the Lord Himself. They are consecrated for the royal priesthood and the holy people (cf. 1 Peter 2:4–10) not only that they may offer spiritual sacrifices in everything they do but also that they may witness to Christ throughout the world. (*Apostolicam Actuositatem* #2)

> But the laity, by their very vocation, seek the kingdom of God by engaging in temporal affairs and by ordering them according to the plan of God. They live in the world, that is, in each and in all of the secular professions and occupations. They live in the ordinary circumstances

of family and social life, from which the very web of their existence is woven. They are called there by God that by exercising their proper function and led by the spirit of the Gospel they may work for the sanctification of the world from within as a leaven. (*Lumen Gentium* #31)

Since they have an active role to play in the whole life of the Church, laymen are not only bound to penetrate the world with a Christian spirit, but are also called to be witnesses to Christ in all things in the midst of human society. (*Gaudium et Spes* 43)

As noted above, a constitutive and defining mark of diaconal ministry ought to be the facilitation of the laity's apostolate of justice to the world.

The deacon's tasks include that of promoting and sustaining the apostolic activities of the laity. (Pope John Paul II, "Deacon Has Many Pastoral Functions" #5, 1993)

. . . the deacon's fundamental ministry is the support of the laity's participation in the apostolic mission of the Church.[10]

. . . deacons lead, inspire, enable and model for other members of the Church what servant leadership can mean in living the demands of Christian discipleship in the contemporary world.[11]

Note the survey of the threefold dignity associated with baptism is silent vis-a-vis the laity's kingly *ad intra* baptismal dignity. As we associate this dimension of baptismal dignity with authority, governance and decision-making, as indicated above, we are left to admit that the current *ad intra* mechanisms and structures of the aforesaid fail to do justice to this dimension of the faithful's baptismal dignity for such mechanisms and structures which would enable the laity to share in ecclesial decision-making are currently lacking in spite of the prolific teachings of the Second Vatican Council calling for such. As we have now seen, the message

10. McKnight, "Deacon as *Medius Ordo*," 84.

11. Ditewig, "Charting a Theology of the Diaconate," 55.

proffered by Vatican II regarding the laity has a twofold emphasis: 1) empowerment for greater participation in the church (*ad intra*), i.e., expanded appreciation of the laity's activity in the church's sacramental life; 2) vibrant mission in the secular world (*ad extra*), i.e., the laity's apostolate of social justice. In both realms—the church and the world—the laity are seen as engaging in activities which build up the church—activities which they are encouraged to initiate and to which they have a right and duty.

> The Lay apostolate, in all its many aspects, is exercised both in the Church and in the world. (*Apostolicam Actuositatem* #9)

> All the laity have the exalted duty of working for the ever greater spread of the divine plan of salvation to all of humanity of every epoch and over all the earth. Therefore may the way be clear for them to share diligently in the salvific work of the Church according to their ability and the needs of the time. (*Lumen Gentium* #33)

The council beseeches bishops and priests to recognize, affirm and work collaboratively with the activities of the laity, while acknowledging equality among ecclesial members (see *Lumen Gentium* #32).

> By reason of the knowledge, competence or pre-eminence which they have the laity are empowered—indeed sometimes obliged—to manifest their opinion on those things which pertain to the good of the Church. (*Lumen Gentium* #37)

> In the Church are to be found very many apostolic enterprises owing their origin to the free choice of the laity and run at their own discretion. Such enterprises enable the Church . . . to fulfill her mission more effectively . . . (*Apostolicam Actuositatem* #24)

> The hierarchy's duty is to favor the lay apostolate . . . (*Apostolicam Actuositatem* #24)

> Bishops, parish priests and other priests of the secular and regular clergy will remember that the right and duty of exercising the apostolate are common to all the

faithful . . . and that in the building up of the Church the laity too have parts of their own to play. (*Apostolicam Actuositatem* #25)

The pastors, indeed, should recognize and promote the dignity and responsibility of the laity in the Church. They should willingly use their prudent advice and confidently assign duties to them in the service of the Church, leaving them freedom and scope for acting. Indeed, they should give them the courage to undertake works on their own initiative. (*Lumen Gentium* #37)

In exercising his office of father and pastor the bishop should be with his people as one who serves . . . In exercising his ministry he should ensure that the faithful are duly involved in Church affairs; he should recognize their right and duty to play their part in building up the Mystical Body of Christ. (*Christus Dominus* #16)

Priests should unite their efforts with those of the lay faithful and conduct themselves among them after the example of the Master who came amongst men not to be served but to serve . . . Priests are to be sincere in their appreciation and promotion of lay people's dignity and of the special role the laity have to play in the Church's mission . . . They should be willing to listen to lay people, give brotherly consideration to their wishes, and recognize their experience and competence in the different fields of human activity. In this way they will be able to recognize along with them the signs of the times. (*Presbyterorum Ordinis* #9)

In *Called and Gifted*, the American Bishop's pastoral letter on the laity, the bishops expand upon the council's vision and call the laity to be adults within the church. Adulthood implies knowledge, experience and awareness, freedom and responsibility, and mutuality in relationships. Adulthood, as understood by the bishops, involves the laity: giving advice to pastors; proposing suggestions and desires to clergy; manifesting their opinion in the life of the church; and proffering their unique knowledge and competence to the service of the church.

We maintain that such affirmation of the adulthood of the laity, along with the church's consistent magisterial teachings regarding democratic forms of governance being most consistent with human dignity, advocacy of subsidiarity (see Appendix), and acknowledgement of the *sensus fidelium* (See *Lumen Gentium* #12), warrant greater ecclesial consideration of future mechanisms of shared governance and decision-making within the church (see *Lumen Gentium* #37). In addition to being consistent with these aforesaid affirmations and teachings, we also maintain that such empowerment of the laity is, likewise, consistent with the *ad intra* kingly and prophetic dignity bestowed upon them by the Lord via baptism (see *Lumen Gentium* #'s 12, 34–35). As previously considered in this book, given historical precedent as well as the contemporary need of the church, deacons could play a significant role in advancing new ecclesial models of governance which ensure that the aforesaid rights of the laity vis-a-vis church leadership are respected and actualized.

Canon law does call for certain lay ecclesial bodies, e.g., parish finance councils and diocesan pastoral councils, but ultimately deem them advisory and/or optional entities. Until new models of ecclesial governance are developed and implemented which honor and respect the *ad intra kingly* baptismal dignity of the laity, and the breadth and scope of the Spirit's gifts shared amongst and operative within the church, then the ecclesiological vision of the Second Vatican Council remains unrealized.

# 5

# Ecclesial *Kenosis* and Diaconal Ministry

THE SECOND VATICAN COUNCIL called for an ecclesial *kenosis*. Via accentuating ecclesiologies which call for the church to be a missionary servant at pilgrimage within the world acting as a sacrament, the council emphasized that the church's mentality, attitude and disposition be marked by a *kenosis* which enabled her to most effectively reach people where they were at:

> Having been divinely sent to the nations that she might be the universal sacrament of salvation the church, in obedience to the command of her founder and because it is demanded by her own essential universality, strives to preach the gospel to all people. (*Ad Gentes* #1)

As such, the council committed the church to an evangelical enterprise that was inclusive and universal in scope:

> The joy and hope, the grief and anguish of the people of our time, especially those who are poor or afflicted in any way, are the joy and hope, the grief and anguish of the followers of Christ as well . . . the Second Vatican Council . . . resolutely addresses not only the children of the church and all who call upon the name of Christ, but the whole of humanity as well, and it longs to set forth

> the way it understands the presence and function of the church in the world of today . . . the world which the Council has in mind is the whole human family seen in the context of everything which envelopes it. (*Gaudium et Spes* #'s 1–2)

Consequently, the church needs to be open to diverse and pluralistic cultures and theological methodologies which enable her to efficaciously point to and make present the love of God in Jesus present among all people. The church's task:

> . . . is one and the same everywhere and in all situations, although because of circumstances, it may not always be exercised in the same way. (*Ad Gentes* #6)

Therefore, no singular theological methodologies nor ecclesial models or articulations (little "t's") of gospel Truths (Big "T's") definitively and exhaustively capture and convey the entirety of the church nor gospel message completely and in its entirety. The church must be willing to empty herself of methodologies, models, articulations and paradigms which fail to resonate with the lived experience of the faithful. The church must *kenotically* open herself to new ways and means of communicating the love of God if she is to be efficacious in her efforts to be a sacrament:

> . . . the Church . . . is not tied exclusively and indissolubly to any race or nation, to any one particular way of life, or to any customary practices, ancient or modern. (*Gaudium et Spes* #58)

God is love. As such, God longs to express himself so as to invite others into relationship and union with him. For this to occur, God gratuitously empties himself so as to reveal himself, enter into salvation history and draw people to himself. God is a *kenotic* God—a God who empties himself in love—so that *theosis*—the divinization of persons (relationship/union with God) is possible. Furthermore, Jesus is the ultimate expression of God's *kenotic* love whereby the Incarnation and his life of *diakonia* God expresses his love in the gift of his son who, in turn, *kenotically* conveyed his love to humanity so as to invite us to relationship and union with the Father (see Philippians 2:6–11 and Matthew 20:25–28).

The *anawim*, i.e., faithful followers who strive to emulate God and Jesus by serving God and others, must be openly disposed to receive God and simultaneously openly disposed to serve others. *Kenotically* emptying themselves, the faithful experience *theosis* as they allow God to permeate their lives (an interior spiritual poverty) and as they go outside of themselves to serve others and therein discover God yet again (see Matthew 25). The spiritual dialectic of the Christian faith is one in which the vertical/transcendent/God, the interior/subjective/self, and the horizontal/service/neighbor are inextricably interconnected whereby an incessant pattern of *kenosis* unto *theosis* unto *diakonia* unfolds.

Diaconal spirituality must therefore evolve from *theosis* with God unto *kenotic* configuration to Christ unto diaconal service to others, for deacons are called to grow in their relationship with God by emptying themselves in service to their bishop, priests, parishioners and to all to whom they are to offer charity. The personalist philosopher Emmanuel Levinas noted that *diakonia*—responsible care for and service unto others—is what enables one to transcend oneself. As we respond to/serve the needs of others we are liberated from our own egos. Therefore, responding to others simultaneously creates a new self. The more one serves others the more one becomes a new self, and this goes on to infinity. Serving others illuminates the infinite/God. Therefore, serving others is the means by which we experience God. Levinas describes diaconal service as a move into "messianic time," i.e., in serving others one does what the messiah would do. *Diakonia*, therefore, entails living as if one is the messiah vis-à-vis the one before oneself in need.[1] "In the diaconate one can see the mystery of how one comes to be human and transcendent through the service of others."[2] Recall that diaconal ordination configures the deacon to Christ the servant of all and that deacons are to be living icons of Christ the servant. Therefore, diaconal *kenosis* is

1. Donovan, *Sacrament of Service*, 26.
2. Ibid., 26.

exercised "not as a simple expression of social justice or social service, but as a way to draw others more fully into the Paschal Mystery of Christ and to guide others to salvation"[3] (see also Matthew 22:36–40; 20:25–28; 25:35–40).

"Blessed are the poor in spirit, for theirs is the kingdom of God" (Matthew 5). The poor in spirit are those who accept Jesus' call to discipleship and who recognize their utter dependency upon God. As such, spiritual poverty entails an inner orientation to God. Being spiritually poor also involves a social orientation and direction. As followers of Jesus the spiritually poor have an obligation to the poor for they are devoted to the one who cares for the needy in all of their needs. Furthermore, the poor, themselves, are blessings for they bear Christ unto us. The Bible contains more than three hundred verses pertaining to the poor and social justice and God's relation to them. God reveals himself as one who takes the needs of the poor to heart; who identifies with the oppressed; and one who calls people to remember the poor with compassion and justice. Spiritual poverty and service of the poor are blessings, indeed, for they illuminate the mystery of God himself. Spiritual poverty is precisely what brings one close to God and which enables one to see that the poor are the ones closest to God's heart.

Poverty in spirit entails a *kenosis* of imagination. For deacons, this means a ministry understood in terms of *munera* not power; availability and flexibility, not selfishness; a pastoral personalist ministerial disposition, not rigid legalism. The more receptive the deacon is of God's love, the more God's love transforms the deacon. To receive God the deacon must empty himself so as to make room for God. Deacons must descend in order to ascend. God must increase, the deacon must decrease. Like Mary, the deacon must *kenotically* empty himself so that God can enter into and be mediated forth from the deacon. Diaconal *kenosis* is a means by which the deacon allows God to indwell and God to communicate the love of Jesus to others. Like Mary's *Fiat* and *Magnificat*, the deacon's own "yes" to God must, likewise, enable God to act through the deacon so that the love and glory of God can be communicated

3. Ditewig, *Emerging Diaconate*, 156.

through him. As Meister Eckhart taught, *kenosis* is the means by which the birth of the son/Jesus can occur within one's soul. Being configured to Jesus via ordination and the charisms it affords, deacons are disposed for this to occur. *Diakonia* seeks to glorify God, not the deacon. "To be spiritually poor is the capacity to endure the pain of receiving love from the Trinity and circulate such love among others."[4] Union with God empowers and animates diaconal service unto others, as it did for Jesus. Jesus' ministry of service was a result of his responding to what he received from God. Jesus', and the deacon's, ministry is a result of what is received from God. *Kenosis* ought to be the definitive characteristic for deacons. *Kenosis* becomes more real and concrete the more one dedicates oneself to service. "Your diaconal ministry commits you to the Christ's own radical availability to those in need . . . That is what the diaconate is in its essence: the consent by one to be drawn into Christ's very being for others."[5] Deacons empty themselves for Jesus' sake. In following Jesus, deacons are called to lose their very selves. They are called to serve others. Deacons are called within the salvific economy of God to minister *in persona Christi servi*, i.e., in the person of Christ the servant. Via their participation in holy orders they are configured to Christ, the deacon and servant of all. Therefore, deacons, like the church at large, are to make God, Jesus and themselves present to all so that the kingdom of God becomes present.

Diaconal service advances God's kingdom. As the diaconal prototypes, Saints Stephen and Philip evidence in their ministries as presented in the Book of Acts (see chapter 1), deacons are to be witnesses unto the saving designs of God offered in and through the person of Jesus, and do so in ways and means that are inclusive, culturally sensitive and universal in scope. Deacons, therefore, evidence for the church in microcosm what she is to be macrocosmically. Deacons are in miniature what the church is to be at large. Deacons witness to the church what it means to be church.

---

4. Keating, *Heart of the Diaconate*, 43.

5. Ibid., 19.

> Through ordination the deacon is empowered . . . with a kenotic power, a power or strength to empty himself in service to the church . . . those who would be leaders in the community of disciples are to be identified by their own self-sacrificing love in imitation of the kenosis of Christ . . .[6]

Greater than the tasks performed or services rendered, *diakonia* is more than functionalism. Diaconal service presupposes an underlying charism and is definitively marked by *kenosis*. Deacons are living exemplars of *kenosis*, icons of Jesus the servant. As such, deacons seek to incarnate the love of Jesus via *diakonia*. Diaconal ministry is to manifest the *kenosis* of Jesus' self-emptying via the surrendering of the deacon's will and love to God and others, and via their praxis in imitation of Jesus the foot washer.

> The ministerial diaconate sacramentalizes the self-emptying love of Christ on behalf of others . . . through the sacramental grace received at ordination the deacon receives the strength to empty himself in the service of others . . .[7]

## Deacons: Servants of Ecumenism and Interreligious Dialogue

Pope John XXIII's vision for the Second Vatican Council committed the church to search for truth and unity with the faithful of all religious communities and recognized such efforts as corresponding to the will of the Divine Redeemer. The pope invited prayers from all Christians and people of good will that the council may also be to their advantage. The pope also invited select non-Catholics to attend/observe the conciliar proceedings and instructed various heads of conciliar commissions to consult with said observers.

Additionally, prior to the council, Pope John XXIII established a new office in 1960 within the Roman Curia—the Secretariat for

---

6. Ditewig, "Charting a Theology of the Diaconate," 44–45.

7. Ditewig, "*Kenotic* Leadership of Deacons," 256.

the Promotion of Christian Unity, headed by Cardinal Augustine Bea—and charged it with keeping the ecumenical priority at the forefront of the council's agenda. As the council unfolded, this office would facilitate the participation of ecumenical observers, advise the pope and various conciliar commissions, and was ultimately empowered to act as a conciliar commission in its own right with the authority to draft documents. Additionally, in 1964 Pope Paul VI created a department within the Roman Curia for relations with people of other religions, originally known as the Secretariat for Non-Christians, and later renamed the Pontifical Council for Interreligious Dialogue in 1988. For popes John and Paul, ecumenism and interreligious dialogue were among the signs of the times which they had to give attention to at the council.

The popes' understanding of the nature and purpose of the council, as articulated above, represent an inspired departure from previous Roman Catholic attitudes and policy toward ecumenical movements, for as the history of ecumenism and interreligious dialogue prior to the Second Vatican Council reveals, ecumenical and interreligious activity on the part of Roman Catholics had very nearly been anathema. Repeatedly, Rome had refused invitations and forbidden participation in early ecumenical conferences.

A foundational principle for Catholicism's new ecumenical and interreligious commitments was the growing acknowledgement that grace and vestiges/elements of the church of Christ were present in other religious communities and, thus, in some measure, those communities participate in the one church of Christ. Furthermore, even as the Catholic Church maintains that the fullness of salvation subsists in the Catholic Church, it nonetheless also recognizes that other churches also have been utilized by the Spirit as means of salvation. Such growth marks a departure from the hitherto tendency of the Catholic Church to equate itself solely with the church of Christ. Additionally, while the Catholic Church will insist that it possesses the fullness of the means of salvation, it will also acknowledge that it is a pilgrim church still growing in Christ and in need of perennial reform, purification and renewal.

Thus, one of the most significant expressions of ecclesial *kenosis* evidenced by the Second Vatican Council was the council's commitment to ecumenism and interreligious dialogue. *Nostra Aetate (Declaration on the Church's Relationship with Non-Christian Religions)* and *Unitatis Redintegratio (Decree on Ecumenism)* represented a true *metanoia* on the part of the church and ushered in a new trajectory in the church's interreligious and ecumenical overtures. The council's commitments to ecumenism and interreligious dialogue mark a departure from the previously prevailing ecclesiologies which tended to be triumphalistic/militant, circumscribed/self-enveloping, exclusive/intolerant, and elitist/non-dialogical. Vatican II opened the church to ecumenism and interreligious dialogue, moving beyond notions that there was no salvation outside the church to acknowledging rays of divine truth, goodness and holiness operative in other religions. The council also acknowledged that God/the Holy Spirit were operative in other religious traditions in ways and means that were not deprived of salvific relevance and importance for "God's providence, evident goodness, and saving designs extend to all persons" (*Nostra Aetate* #1) for God wishes all people to be saved (see *Ad Gentes* #7).

> The Catholic Church rejects nothing of what is true and holy in other religions ... She has high regard for the manner of life and conduct, precepts and doctrines ... which reflect a ray of truth which enlightens all people ... The Church, therefore, urges ... discussion and collaboration with members of other religions. (*Nostra Aetate* # 2)

> ... all who have been justified by faith in baptism are incorporated into Christ ... many of the most significant elements and endowments which together go to build up and give life to the Church can exist outside the ... Catholic Church ... The brethren divided from us also carry out many liturgical actions of the Christian religion ... these liturgical actions most certainly can truly engender a life of grace and ... can aptly give access to the communion of salvation ... It follows that the separated Churches and communities ... have been by no means deprived of significance and importance in the

mystery of salvation. For the Spirit of Christ has not re-
frained from using them as means of salvation. (*Unitatis
Redintegratio* #3)

In the words of Saint Pope John Paul II, "at the Second Vatican Council the Catholic Church committed herself irrevocably to
following the path of the ecumenical venture" (Pope John Paul II,
*Ut Unum Sint* #3, 1995), for the church posited that:

> The restoration of unity among all Christians is one of
> the principal concerns of the Second Vatican Council
> ... division openly contradicts the will of Christ, scan-
> dalizes the world, and damages the most holy cause, the
> preaching of the Gospel to every creature ... It is the
> Council's urgent desire that every effort should be made
> toward the gradual realization of this unity ... (*Unitatis
> Redintegratio* #'s 1 and 18)

In remarkable expressions of ecclesial *kenosis*, Vatican II proffered
an admission of guilt on the part of the Roman church for historical Christian divisions (see *Unitatis Redintegratio* #'s 3, 7, 17) and
acknowledged that "sometimes one tradition has come nearer to a
full appreciation of some aspects of a mystery of revelation than the
other, or has expressed them better" (*Unitatis Redintegratio* #17).
Conveying incredible *kenotic* humility, the council challenged the
church, "when comparing doctrines with one another they should
remember that in Catholic doctrine there exists a hierarchy of
truths, since they vary in their relation to the foundation of the
Christian faith" (*Unitatis Redintegratio* #11).

Such a disposition vis-à-vis other religions was seen by the
council fathers as a constitutive aspect of the council's wider
ecclesiology. If the church is to be a servant unto all of humanity, committed to revealing the love, goodness, holiness and truth
of God to all people, it only makes sense that she would seek to
be in solidarity with all peoples of faith and good will. To be an
agent of solidarity and efficacious sacrament, the establishment
of bonds with others who, likewise, strive to make God known is
necessary, otherwise the ecclesiological enterprise proffered by the
council is compromised/undermined. Therefore, the council calls

all Christians to prayer and an interior conversion which would open the minds and change the attitudes of all so that they might be open to unity (see *Unitatis Redintegratio* #7). Via dialogue, all Christians are called to learn from other believers so that one may share their faith with others and receive the faith of others so that via such a dialogical dialectic of one's understanding of God matures and is edified (see *Unitatis Redintegratio* #9).

> But the plan of salvation also includes those who acknowledge the Creator. Nor is God far distant from those who in shadows and images seek the unknown God, for it is He who gives to all men life and breath and all things, and as Savior wills that all men be saved. Those also can attain to salvation who through no fault of their own do not know the Gospel of Christ or His Church, yet sincerely seek God and moved by grace strive by their deeds to do His will as it is known to them through the dictates of conscience. Nor does Divine Providence deny the helps necessary for salvation to those who, without blame on their part, have not yet arrived at an explicit knowledge of God and with His grace strive to live a good life. (*Lumen Gentium* #16)

> The Second Vatican Council, centered primarily on the theme of the Church, reminds us of the Holy Spirit's activity also "outside the visible body of the Church." The Council speaks precisely of "all people of good will in whose hearts grace works in an unseen way. For, since Christ died for all, and since the ultimate vocation of man is in fact one, and divine, we ought to believe that the Holy Spirit in a manner known only to God offers to every man the possibility of being associated with this Paschal Mystery." (Pope John Paul II, *Dominum et Vivicantem* #53)

> . . . God shows no partiality. Rather, the person of any nation who fears God and acts uprightly is acceptable to him. (Acts 10:34–35)

Via their personal lives, secular work, ministerial apostolates and sacramental presidency and assistance, deacons are well positioned within the church to advance her commitment to ecumenism and interreligious dialogue. Therefore, "a genuine ecumenism should be thoroughly incorporated into all aspects of diaconal formation" (United States Conference of Catholic Bishops, *National Directory* #151, 2005). Families and work places today are increasingly more diverse and pluralistic as our world becomes more interconnected. Being at home in these two spheres, deacons are able to draw from their family and work experiences ecumenical and interreligious understandings and sensitivities into their ministry. Perhaps their child takes a Muslim to prom, or has a Jew as a good friend with whom the child socializes and even satisfies high school service hours requirements with by spending a summer volunteering at the local Jewish community center. Perhaps the deacon's wife works at an elementary school which is 70 percent Hindu and whose colleagues are Protestant, Muslim and Hindu. Perhaps their child at college roommates with an evangelical Protestant at a university in the south. Perhaps the deacon's own superiors, colleagues or neighbors are persons of different faiths. Such experiences can do much to inform and edify a deacon's ministry when he is assigned prison ministry as an apostolate, presides over inter-faith marriages or funerals, or is called upon to conduct ecumenical and interreligious events at his parish. Such occasions are opportune moments for the deacon to convey the church's ecumenical and interreligious commitments in a manner informed and substantiated by their own lived experiences.

## Deacons: Instruments of Peace

The Second Vatican Council can be said to have advanced a new ecclesial attitude toward war attributed to the pope who convened the council, Pope John XXIII. Beginning with Pope John's encyclical, *Pacem in Terris*, the church began to move away from a disposition that tended to justify war toward a commitment to peace as a process.

> In an age such as ours . . . it is contrary to reason to hold
> that war is now a suitable way to restore rights which
> have been violated. (Pope John XXIII, *Pacem in Terris*
> #127, 1963)

The pope who brought the council to conclusion, Paul VI, echoed
such sentiments:

> No more war, war never again. It is peace, peace which
> must guide the destinies of peoples and of all mankind.
> (Pope Paul VI, "Address to the United Nations," 1965)

Given the advent of modern weapons which are capable of de-
struction that is indiscriminate in scope and breadth, the church
has increasingly questioned whether or not war remains a legitimate moral option. Coupled with the exorbitant expense associated with military stockpiling and budgets, the potential adverse
ecological impacts of modern weapons, and the inherent blow to
trust spawned by arms races, the church suggests that there be a
new attitude towards war (see *Gaudium et Spes* #'s 79–81). Indeed,
the council asserted that "it is our clear duty to spare no effort in
order to work for the moment when all war will be completely
outlawed . . ." (*Gaudium et Spes* #82).

The church, however, has not gone so far as to definitively out-
law all war so long as the requisite conditions for peace are lacking,
for "peace is more than the absence of war . . . it is appropriately
called the effect of righteousness . . . peace is also the fruit of love,
for love goes beyond what justice can ensure" (*Gaudium et Spes*
# 78). An absence of global economic and political cooperation
impedes the process of peace. Christians, therefore, have a duty to
work for the creation and establishment of social, economic and
political entities committed to solidarity. Even if war has not been
completely outlawed, the church further gave voice to its disdain
for war by giving renewed voice to the option of pacifism. The demands of justice and the common good require Christian action.
The nature of said action, however, need not necessitate recourse to
violence. Pacifism is a legitimate Christian option.

Deacons are uniquely positioned within the church to serve as instruments of peace. Something that has struck me over the course of my twenty-five years of teaching deacons and their wives is the significant number of the men who either are serving or have served in the military, both in enlisted and civilian capacities. This phenomena is such a regular occurrence that I have often reflected upon how and why this is the case. There is an obvious correlation between military service and the diaconate in that both evidence a willingness to respond to the call to serve for a community and cause greater than oneself. Furthermore, like the church, the military is hierarchically structured. Although every deacon, indeed every Christian, is called to imitate the prince of peace, those deacons who have military experiences have much to teach the church about peace. Their experiences and knowledge are invaluable to the church as she continues to reflect upon modern war and the process of peace. Deacons who are also military have a unique perspective on how "peacemaking is the living strand that the diaconate weaves within the tapestry of the Church."[8] Said deacons are uniquely positioned to be heralds of the message proffered in Ephesians 2:14–18, i.e., that it is Jesus who makes peace possible by breaking down barriers of hostility which divide us by making us one in God via his message of reconciliation and gift of the Spirit which enable peace to be possible. We are well served in our efforts to advance the church's new attitude towards war to make the prayer of St. Francis of Assisi (historically associated with the diaconate) our own prayer.

> Lord, make me an instrument of your peace.
> Where there is hatred, let me sow love;
> where there is injury, pardon;
> where there is doubt, faith;
> where there is despair, hope;
> where there is darkness, light;
> and where there is sadness, joy.

8. Keating, "Moral Life of the Deacon," 126.

O Divine Master, grant that I may not so much seek
to be consoled as to console;
to be understood as to understand;
to be loved as to love.
For it is in giving that we receive;
it is in pardoning that we are pardoned;
and it is in dying that we are born to eternal life. Amen.

Peace begins with an interior conversion which, in turn, extends to relationships. Responding to the call of the diaconate bespeaks of interior conversion and, therefore, as a public vocation within the church has the potential of providing others a lived witness of interior conversion which, in turn, *kenotically* re-orientates oneself to relationships with others marked by the example of Jesus, the embodiment of peace. Additionally, reconciliation is to be a hallmark of peace. As previously discussed, the scope and breadth of a deacon's relationships and ministries (cleric, husband, father, co-worker, minister) challenge deacons to be agents and models of interpersonal reconciliation. As such, by the witness of their lives, deacons are able to manifest unto the church what reconciliation is to look like. In short, deacons are capable of being examples of peace within the church *ad intra* as well as instruments extending the church's peace of Jesus *ad extra*.

## Deacons: Champions of Human Dignity

*Gaudium at Spes, The Pastoral Constitution on the Church in the Modern World*, proffers the anthropological vision of the Second Vatican Council, i.e., a Christian vision of the human person. Said document posits that human beings are: the image and likeness of God (see *Gaudium et Spes* #12); rational and spiritual (see *Gaudium et Spes* #'s 14, 15, 18, 19); loving (see *Guadium et Spes* #12); free (see *Gaudium et Spes* #17); and interpersonal/ communitarian (see *Gaudium et Spes* #'s 12, 6, 24, 25). Created by God as such, the council maintained that all cultural, social, political and economic realities must respect and allow for the expression, development and advancement of each/all of these innate characteristics which are sacrosanct and inviolate. To do otherwise is not only a crime against human beings, but a sin before God. Additionally, the council asserted that Christians must prove themselves to be signs of communitarian unity within the world in which we live (see *Gaudium et Spes* # 27). This means that the church must demonstrate an unyielding commitment to the intrinsic dignity, value and worth of every human being and evidence how human divisions can be overcome. Frequently this means that the church will have to be a prophetic counter-cultural witness.

From the aforesaid one can discern how the council's anthropological vision balances the dignity and rights of the individual vis-à-vis a commitment to the common good, i.e., "the sum total of social conditions which allow people, either as groups or as individuals, to reach their fulfilment more fully and more easily" (*Gaudium et Spes* #'s 26, 74, 78). The principles outlined in Catholic Social Teaching provide the road map for constructing cultural, social, political and economic realities which preserve such a balance between individuals and the common good. The council offered a summation of Catholic Social Teaching and maintained that it is each Christian's task to work for a more just society based on truth, justice, love and freedom. The Conciliar teaching sums up nearly a century of Catholic Social Thought. Obviously, the church judges that the most appropriate form of living is a manner that is in conformity with the spirit of the gospel. Justice and charity are hallmarks of the gospel message. Therefore the council espoused a communitarian social vision informed by its anthropology and Catholic Social Teaching by asserting that the aim of human activity is to be human beings (see *Gaudium et Spes* #26), i.e., that human beings are "the source, focus and end of all economic and social life" (*Gaudium et Spes* #63). Subsidiarity (see *Gaudium et Spes* #'s 69, 86), distributive justice and concern for social, political and economic balance (see *Gaudium et Spes* #'s 29, 63, 66, 69) are deemed to be requisites for any just ordering of society, as is a preferential option for the poor. Economic justice is said to require that the worker take precedence over capital and technology (see

*Gaudium et Spes* #'s 35, 67); a just wage (see *Gaudium et Spes* #67); and the right to associate (see *Gaudium et Spes* #68). Furthermore, the council posited that "political justice demands that all citizens have the right and the duty to contribute to the genuine progress of their community" (*Gaudium et Spes* #65). Only if these aspects are recognized and respected can human dignity and the common good be successfully promoted and solidarity among peoples be realized (see *Gaudium et Spes* #'s 24, 57). All of the aforesaid presumes the exercise of responsible stewardship (see *Gaudium et Spes* #34) vis-à-vis the goods of creation.

We have already considered in previous chapters how deacons can advance this anthropological and social vision of the Second Vatican Council via their unique preaching and teaching roles within the life of the church, via supporting lay apostolates, and via the lived witness of their own lives. Indeed, a particular obligation of the church is to conscientisize persons so as to inspire action. However, if this anthropological and social vision of the council is to be more fully realized, then diaconal ministries are going to have to be even more readily and prolifically at the service of ecclesial ministries dedicated to the dignity and sanctity of human life, sociopolitical and economic justice, and environmental and ecological ethics. Abortion, capital punishment, euthanasia, sexual exploitation, excessive capitalism, wage disparity, economic disparity, political marginalization, immigration, prejudice and discrimination, pollution, global warming, etc., etc., are issues plaguing our contemporary society. The church must lend her prophetic voice to these causes for, as the council committed, the church must be about the healing and elevation of human dignity, the building and consolidation of bonds of solidarity, and the endowment of daily human activity with deeper meaning and worth. Therefore, deacons who are able to draw upon experiences and competencies relevant and pertinent to these challenges due to their particular stations and calls of life must interweave these experiences and competencies more intentionally and deliberately into their ecclesial ministerial responsibilities, duties and service. Such will require diaconal courage for prophetic witness often has social, political and economic implications.

## Diaconal Ministry and Pastoral Counseling: Deacons as Agents of God's Mercy

Another seminal document promulgated by the council which illuminates the church's anthropological vision is the council's Document on Human Dignity, *Dignitatis Humanae*. Common with *Gaudium et Spes*, *Dingitatis Humanae* gives specific attention to the inviolate sanctity of conscience as a constitutive dimension of humanity being in the image and likeness of God. The Catholic tradition understands conscience to be the ultimate subjective norm of morality, i.e., the highest moral authority to which one is bound, for it marks a uniquely human characteristic and informs our notion of what it is meant to be created in the image and likeness of God.

> In the depths of his conscience, man detects a law which he does not impose upon himself, but which holds him to obedience. Always summoning him to love good and avoid evil, the voice of conscience when necessary speaks to his heart: do this, shun that. For man has in his heart a law written by God; to obey it is the very dignity of man; according to it he will be judged. Conscience is the most secret core and sanctuary of a man. There he is alone with God, Whose voice echoes in his depths. In a wonderful manner conscience reveals that law which is fulfilled by love of God and neighbor. (*Gaudium et Spes* #16)

> The Vatican Council declares that the human person has a right to religious freedom. Freedom of this kind means that all persons should be immune from coercion on the part of individuals, social groups and every human power so that nobody is forced to act against their convictions in religious matters . . . The Council further declares that the right to religious freedom is based in the very dignity of the human person . . . It is through one's conscience that one sees and recognizes the demands of the divine law. One is bound to follow this conscience faithfully in all of their activity so that they may come to God, Who is their last end. Therefore, one must not be forced to act contrary to their conscience. Nor must

one be prevented from acting in accord with one's conscience, especially in religious matters . . . to deny one
the free exercise of religion . . . is to do an injustice to the
human person and to the very order established by God
. . . (*Dignitatis Humanae* #'s 2–3; #10)

Scripture also speaks of conscience as God's voice calling from
within. Conscience is one's innermost being where one is called to
fidelity to God and to the covenant. It is the Spirit of God within the
person guiding the person. Again, Scripture captures this understanding in its vision of the heart. The heart not only accuses one
subsequent to doing wrong, it also leads one to listen to the Spirit
and its promptings and illumination (see Jeremiah 31:29–34; Eze-
kiel 14:1–3; 36:26). St. Paul fortified the biblical notion of the heart,
further enriching the dynamic presence of the Spirit by describing
conscience as not only an inner remorse/voice of accusation, but
also the creative quality of one to grasp what is good and right in
advance of decisions (see Romans 2:14–15).

In light of such teachings, we can see that conscience is deter-
minative of our very character—who we are. Our character reflects
the value system/stories/narratives which have influenced us and
that inform our moral deliberations. In chapter 4 we considered
how character determines our vision—the way we see the world
(worldview)—which, in turn, informs our imagination, choices,
decisions and actions. In short, character, as an expression of conscience, reveals our attitudes, dispositions and orientation toward
that which we direct our freedom. Diaconal ministry ought to be
directed toward the formation of people's character(s).

Conscience and character are formed within the context of
communities which proffer various stories/narratives and their
intrinsic value systems. Diaconal ministry is a vehicle by which
the church can share the church's story/narrative/traditions/
teachings in the process of contributing to one's process of informing their conscience/forming their character. A deacon's task is to
share ecclesial stories and to assist in the process of conscience
and character formation, not to dictate courses of action. Indeed,
a deacon ought to consider if his ministry either draws others to

the sacramental life of the church—the ecclesial economy in which our narratives, ritual and symbols are enacted and lived out—or drives them away from this treasure of the church.

Although consultation and consideration of the church's teaching is requisite to the process of forming one's conscience/character, the ultimate decision regarding moral courses of action is to be determined by the individual as he/she strives to discern what they must do in a particular situation. Catholic tradition maintains that one is always bound to follow one's conscience. Even if conscience errs, it does not lose its dignity. Thus, an erroneous dictate of conscience obliges one in the same way as a correct conscience. A deacon's task is to help others understand the gospel values and to foster their assimilation, not to determine their specific application for individuals. It would be a serious fault against the dignity of conscience if one were to press one to act against their conscience, or force one to inculcate an objective norm if doing so would usurp one's conscience.

The Second Vatican Council declared that the human person has a right to religious freedom and that this right is based on the very dignity of the human person (see *Dignitatis Humanae* #'s 2, 10). Furthermore, the council taught that this freedom precludes any/all forms of coercion which would force one to act contrary to their convictions, or prevent one from acting in accordance with their convictions in religious matters—one's response to God ought to be free (see *Dignitatis Humanae* #'s 2, 10). In short, when making moral judgments there is no higher authority than conscience. There is no authority that can over-ride/usurp the personal judgment of conscience. Additionally, conscience is not accessible to anyone but the individual. Therefore, no other person has the right or ability to judge the integrity of another person's judgment of conscience. It is a sin against the very nature of the person to urge them to violate their conscience. As summarized by the moral theologian James P. Hanigan,

> No external authority should be preferred to the judgment of one's own conscience. Not only do human beings have the moral right to follow their own consciences; it

is also their most fundamental and solemn moral obligation to do so.[9]

Diaconal ministry ought to assist in the process of conscience formation. Although one's conscience is fallible, it remains the ultimate moral authority. Deacons must share the church's teachings as authoritative dimensions within the process of conscience formation, but must avoid judging others when they act according to their conscience, even if they are wrong. Deacons must avoid dictating actions as they would like them to be. They must continue to love the other as one is loved by Christ (*agape/kenosis*). Deacons are to use moral rules to share accumulated and preserved wisdom; to facilitate deliberation; as prods/correctives; to invite to the common good; but, most of all, in the service of love and relationships.

Ours is a pilgrim ethic, a pilgrim tradition, and, as we have seen, we are a pilgrim church (see chapter 3). Our openness to the Spirit demands that we allow ourselves to be remade and our nature transformed (see Romans 12:12). Such adaptation requires that we discern what the Spirit is saying to us in the here and now, i.e., what God is calling us to do at this specific time within this specific context. A deacon's task ought to be to assist others in the discernment process. Discernment is not facilitated by mechanically and woodenly imposing a scheme of analysis onto another. Such an approach would be experienced as external by others, i.e., imposed from the outside. Discernment involves more than arranging teachings in a logical and orderly way. Such an approach fails to perceive the complexities and details of a particular instance. Discernment involves more than the accumulation of relevant information/teachings. One must be able to perceive relationships between aspects of information garnered and how these fit together with the matter at hand, i.e., the ability to draw inferences and expand one's imaginative capacities. Expressive articulation of approval or disapproval does not facilitate discernment. Discernment must entail thoughtful discrimination between values that compete for actualization,

9. Hanigan, *As I Have Loved You*, 139.

between consequences of possible courses of action. Discernment is more than stubborn allegiance to given bases for judgments. It requires sensitivity and flexibility, i.e., pluralistic interpretations in the midst of complicated situations—perceiving what is morally fitting in a given time and place. Discernment must involve a reading of the situation, depth of interpretation and assessment of the pertinent facts, including the history and non-rational aspects of a person that have determined how they perceive a situation, and how the current situation is related to other situations. Discernment is what we pilgrims do while we journey. The aim, goal and purpose of discernment is to deepen our relationship with the Lord. Jesus told his followers that they were his friends (see John 15:9–15). Discernment is directed toward becoming friends with Jesus. A deacon's ministry ought to be one of service unto others in their efforts to befriend Jesus. Deacons are best able to do this if they, themselves, befriend the ones they serve.[10]

Such ministerial friendship requires that deacons share the interests of those whom they serve. Knowing the interests of others demands that one have compassion for them. It requires that one respect that freedom is a prerequisite for friendship—those who are served must freely and willingly embrace the relationship. Coercion and compulsion are contradictory to friendship. Indeed, one of the joys of friendship is the freedom to be oneself with the other; the freedom to speak or be silent; the freedom to come or go, laugh or cry, succeed or fail . . . without imperiling the relationship. This pattern of friendship marked by the respect of the freedom of the other is the example of Jesus. Jesus invited others to relationship while respecting their freedom. While rejection saddened him, it did not lead to recriminations or threats. Ministerial friendship also requires that we respect that there is equality amongst friends. Respecting such equality lends to a dynamic of empowering the other, rather than exerting dominion over others. Friendship requires mercy. Friends must be willing to forgive.[11] A deacon's attitude/disposition

10. See Gula, *Reason Informed by Faith*, 314–29; and Hanigan, *As I Have Loved You*, 209–27.

11. See Hanigan, *As I Have Loved You*, 209–27.

towards others ought to be marked by humility and an awareness that, as the Our Father articulates, we will be forgiven according to the measure which we forgive others.

The late saint and pope, John Paul II, devoted one of his earliest encyclicals to a consideration of God's mercy (*Dives in Misericordia*, 1980). In this work, the pope, speaking of the mercy of God in the mission of the church, posited:

> The church of our time . . . must become more particularly and profoundly conscious of the need to bear witness in her whole mission to God's mercy . . . seeking to introduce it and to make it incarnate in the lives of her faithful . . . (John Paul II, *Dives in Misericordia* #12)

As proclaimer of God's mercy, it is a deacon's task to profess this mercy, not to ensure comprehension of the perfection of the mysterious/inscrutable essence of God but, rather, to facilitate an encounter with the living God. A deacon best serves this function by directing himself and others to the heart of Jesus, for the heart of Jesus makes known the love, forgiveness and mercy of the Father. God's mercy is infinite and inexhaustible . . . as is His readiness to receive prodigal children who return to Him. "No human sin can prevail over this power or even limit it" (*Dives in Misericordia* #13)!

The pope associates the church's ministry of mercy with the perpetual status of conversion that is to be the mark of each/every Christian disciple. By serving as agents of God's mercy, deacons illuminate the tender love of God, the inexhaustible source of conversion—not only conversion as a singular interior act, but as an attitude and state of mind which is to be the mark of the faith pilgrimage. Hence, conversion is to be viewed as an evangelical process, a continuous discovery of love, not a once and for all transformation.

Deacons are charged by Christ, himself, to put mercy into practice. The Beatitudes are a call to action: "Blessed are the merciful, for they shall obtain mercy" (Matthew 5:7). Diaconal ministry ought to be marked by humility, for the dynamic of sharing God's mercy is a reciprocal one, not unilateral. It is only by offering mercy that we, too, receive mercy. Only when ministry is exercised in such a dialectical way does an appropriate equality emerge between persons, an equality which, in turn, propagates mutual love and mercy and fosters spiritual kinship.

As such, ministry and pastoral counseling calls the deacon to more than rendering justice. Rather, justice must be corrected by love and mercy—love and mercy that are patient and kind. Forgiveness, not judgment, bespeaks to the world the love and mercy that is more powerful than sin. Forgiveness, not judgment, is the fundamental condition for reconciliation. It is precisely in the name of love and mercy that Jesus calls us to forgive. Christ so emphasized the need to forgive that he instructed Peter to forgive everyone every time (see Matthew 18:22), and made the extent and degree of our own forgiveness of others the benchmark by which we, ourselves, will be forgiven by God (see Matthew 6:14).

Diaconal ministry involves the responsibility of being grounded in theology—a responsibility which, in turn, renders deacons stewards of the church's tradition and teachings (see chapter 2). Furthermore, as such stewards, diaconal ministry requires that deacons share what they know with the faithful in a manner that is pastorally helpful and life-giving. Ministry and counseling are not about oneself and what one knows, they are about using what one knows to serve others in a manner that helps to illuminate how the faith, tradition and teachings of the church can be meaningful and viable in the life of the one who approaches. Pastoral care and responses will have to be as unique and diverse as the ones who approach. As such, deacons are called to counsel/minister to the faithful in a manner that is pastorally responsible. There is no place for mean spirited use of theology in counseling/ministry! The faith is not a weapon! Rather, a deacon's theological foundation ought to inform and empower him as a witness unto the forgiving, reconciling and merciful nature of our God. Such is the ministerial example of Jesus!

Pope John Paul II asserted that "the diaconate is the church's service sacramentalized." As a sacramental expression of Jesus the servant, diaconal ministry is challenged to be a symbol that points to and makes present the *kenotic* service of Jesus. Such a challenge, again, reminds one that one's ministry is not to be about oneself or what one knows, rather it demands that one radically empty oneself so as to categorically and completely love others so as to invite them to a relationship with God. Diaconal ministry, therefore, ought to be characterized by familial assistance toward enabling one to hear—not oneself—but God.

> Spiritual care is part of a special mission within diakonia. It is related to proclamation but not identical to it . . . In the process of spiritual care as diakonia our task is to listen and to allow the other to talk. Our duty in this form of spiritual care may be to be silent for a long period of time in order to become free of all "priestly" behavior and conceited clericalism. That silence, which is an unconditional prerequisite for spiritual care aids our preaching, for only after a long period of listening is one able to preach appropriately.[12]

In addition to listening, spiritual care must be characterized by the humility of Jesus the servant, and prayer. What one is able to do for another person will be revealed in prayer. Prayer empowers one and those whom one serves to be open to God. Prayer enables one to hear God's word and the stories of our faith which, in turn, can shape one's moral attitudes and stimulate one's moral imagination, i.e., enable one to assimilate the stories of the faith as the framework for one's own personal story and thus form one's moral dispositions, intentions and interpretive context. Humility and prayer make one aware that one's task is not to bind anyone to oneself, to one's opinions, one's judgments at any stage . . . but only to the word and Spirit of Jesus.

The richness, depth and complexity of the Catholic tradition resists oversimplification and a mere deontological approach to ministerial counseling. The tradition and teachings of the church are more than simple rules and regulations that must be obeyed/followed. Rather, they are treasures meant to illuminate truth and foster relationship with God, i.e., shed light on the complex and complicated moral issues/dilemmas that we all contend with, drawing

---

12. Bonhoeffer, *Spiritual Care*, 31.

us toward the will of God. Tradition and church teaching ought to inform the discernment process of the faithful, facilitate their moral judgments, and invite them into greater intimacy with and love for God and others. Diaconal counseling/ministry must mirror the pastoral example of Jesus which went beyond the exacting of justice, to relationship-building and facilitation of the conversion process via fostering love and mercy. Such fidelity to the example of Jesus, in turn, evidences the Pneumatology, ecclesiology and moral theology which mark the church of the Second Vatican Council. The ministerial/counseling approach of deacons ought to take its cue from the ministerial example of Jesus. Jesus was a teacher of wisdom. Wisdom concerns how to live and tends to differentiate between "two ways"—the wise and foolish—and tends to take two different forms of expression: 1) conventional wisdom which expresses a culture's understanding about what is real and how to live; 2) subversive/alternative wisdom which undermines conventional wisdom so as to accentuate another way/path.[13] Jesus' employed parables (short stories) and aphorisms (short, memorable sayings; one liners) to express his wisdom teachings. Jesus' teachings are invitational and provocative—calling upon hearers to see something they might not otherwise see; and evocative in the sense that they call upon the imagination so as to transform one's perception.[14] Jesus' teachings demand further reflection so that new insights are brought to light. The longer parables are narratives employed by Jesus which could be adapted/modified depending upon what a certain occasion warranted. As narratives, these draw one into the story. The stories do not teach via issuing imperatives or by appealing to authority but, rather, by inviting one to allow the story to affect one's imagination so that they can see things in a radically new way. The emphasis upon seeing (*zeteo*) runs through Jesus' message.[15] How we see matters and determines how we choose, act and live. This is the point of Jesus' teachings—to invite others to a new way of living.

13. See Borg, *Meeting Jesus Again*, 69–85.
14. Ibid., 69–85.
15. Ibid., 71–75.

The great parables presented in Luke's Gospel—the Good Samaritan and Prodigal Son—illuminate such an understanding of and approach to pastoral ministry/counseling. In each case traditionally held tenets of morality are re-cast by Jesus in a manner to facilitate relationships with God. Conventional understandings and strict application to moral teachings are usurped by Jesus as he conveys that what is important are not the teachings *per se*, rather it's the manner by which such teachings can be understood, embraced and expressed in the life of the faithful in a manner that facilitates a relationship with God and neighbor. Jesus' ethic is about the kinds of persons we become. The manner of Jesus' ministering/counseling both meets people where they are and moves them toward a process of conversion. It is worth noting that those who are unable to grasp the relational dynamic of Jesus' ethic—those who rigidly adhere to and insist upon the enforcement of strict moral regulations/prescripts—are the ones who ultimately find themselves wedded to their fixed notions and absolutes at the cost of relationships with God and others. Some of Jesus' most severe words are directed via woes against persons (see Matthew 23) because of their rigid interpretation/application of laws/rules/regulations!

Conventional wisdom is the dominant consciousness of any culture—the taken for granted understandings about the way things are, i.e., its worldview and ethos. It represents what we are socialized into as we mature—cultures' social construction of reality which we internalize, i.e., our inculturated consciousness.[16] Conventional wisdom provides guidance about how we are to live; it embodies the central values of a culture. It frequently operates according to the dynamic of reward and punishment.[17] Conventional wisdom has both social and psychological implications: socially it creates a world of hierarchy and boundaries determined by inheritance or performance; psychologically it serves as the basis for our self-identity and self-esteem, internalized by our superego.[18] In its religious form, conventional wisdom tends to present God

16. Ibid., 75.
17. Ibid., 76–77.
18. Ibid., 76–77.

as lawgiver and judge—the one whose requirements must be met and the one who we must satisfy. Religion tends to become a life of requirements. Religion also tends to divide between those who follow conventional wisdom and those who do not.[19]

As a teacher of wisdom, Jesus undermined conventional wisdom and spoke of an alternative. Unlike most teachers who posited that the way of the wise was marked by conformity to conventional wisdom and folly as departing from conventional wisdom, Jesus did the opposite—He tended to directly attack conventional wisdom, frequently doing so by employing paradox and reversal.[20] Jesus invites us to see God as merciful, gracious and compassionate, not as the judge with requirements. He invites us to consider what God is like. Jesus' image of God undermines the dynamic of requirements and rewards at the core of conventional wisdom. The alternative wisdom of Jesus is an invitation to see God as merciful, an invitation to a path of living centered upon God rather than conventional wisdom. Such a path leads to a deepened relationship with the Spirit of God rather than a life of requirements and rewards. It calls for a new heart, an internal transformation, conversion, brought about by a centering upon God. It calls one to a religion based upon relationship with God rather than upon what one has heard/been told. Jesus spoke of the Spirit as the source of renewal and life. The Spirit teaches of Christ, instructing the believer of what pertains to God (see John 14:26 and 1 Corinthians 2:10–15). The Spirit aids us in our weakness interceding for and leading us to prayer and relationship with God (see Romans 8:14, 26–27), rendering us adopted children of God. The early church interpreted Jesus' message regarding the Spirit as entailing ministry that served to safeguard freedom so that the Christian life could be led by the Spirit to actions beyond conventional norms so as to better love and serve others (see 2 Corinthians 3:17; Galatians 4–5; Luke 11:39–46; Acts 15:28).

Contemporary moral theology, likewise, speaks of basic or transcendental freedom, i.e., freedom that not only enables one to decide freely on particular acts, but also the freedom to

19. Ibid., 76.
20. Ibid., 80–81.

determine oneself as a person. Particular acts do not constitute the whole person. The free self-commitment of oneself is more than any particular action and more than the sum of them. One's basic freedom should not be equated with any particular moral act. Basic freedom is the realization of a person as a whole. Basic freedom should not be confused with freedom of choice in particular acts.[21] Scripture captures this notion of basic freedom via its concept of the heart.

Also, there may be impediments to one's freedom. Impediments located in the situation in which one finds oneself are traditionally called actual impediments.[22] A second kind of impediments to human freedom lie within the condition of the moral agent. These impediments are traditionally called habitual or virtual impediments and are rooted in one's psychology, personality, capacities and character features.[23] For an act to be a human act, and not just the act of a human, it must be a free act born out of reflexive, self-aware consciousness.[24]

When one morally assesses human acts one must discern if one's freedom had been impeded, and if one had the requisite conditions to act freely: space (the opportunity to do what one wishes to do and the absence of factors preventing one from acting as one wishes); power (the ability to act so as to achieve one's desired purpose); and authority (the understanding of what is right and what ought to be done).[25] In diaconal ministry and counseling deacons ought not presume that the acts of others were authentically free, i.e., deacons ought to be sensitive to how one's freedom may have been impeded.

Furthermore, in the early church discernment of the Spirit was both a communal as well as individual gift (see 1 Corinthians 12:4–11).

---

21. See Hanigan, *As I Have Loved You*, 53–57.

22. Ibid., 54–55.

23. Ibid., 55.

24. Ibid., 50–53.

25. Ibid., 57–62.

There is only one Spirit who, according to His own richness and the needs of ministries, gives His different gifts for the welfare of the Church . . . this same Spirit produces and stimulates love among the faithful. From this it follows that if one member suffers anything, all the members suffer with him, and if one member is honored, all the members together rejoice. (*Lumen Gentium* #7)

The Holy Spirit . . . gives the faithful special gifts, allotting them to each as He wills so that each and all may put them to the service of others . . . for the building up of the whole body . . . From the reception of these charisms, even the most ordinary ones, there arises for each of the faithful the right and duty of exercising them in the Church and in the world . . . of exercising them in the freedom of the Holy Spirit who breathes where He wills. (*Apostolicam Actuositatem* #3)

Contemporary moral theology describes the individual-communal dynamic operative in the discernment of the Spirit as reciprocity of consciences.[26] Indeed, it is true that a strictly individual concept of conscience is alien to Scripture. However, it is also true that Scripture bespeaks of individual and communal consciences in prophetic engagement with one another. Furthermore, one's conscience does not receive so much light and impulse from laws as from exemplary persons who live truthfully under the authority of their own conscience while respecting the consciences of others. A mature Christian conscience does not think of faith as a catalogue of formulations. A mere articulation of various doctrines without a synthesis in Christ does nothing to help the formation of a distinctively Christian conscience. Indeed, over-emphasis on control and doctrines, and a militant theology, can become an obstacle to an integrated, relational and holistic faith. Whoever gives first place to law and moral obligation while assigning a second place to the grace of Christ perverts the right order and undermines the authenticity of a Christian conscience.[27]

26. Gula, *Reason Informed by Faith*, 137.

27. See Hanigan, *As I Loved You*, 121–25, 139–41; and Gula, *Reason Informed by Faith*, 130, 161.

Moral teaching becomes Good News only if it is presented as an integrated part of faith experience.

The pneumatology and ecclesiology of Vatican II preserve the individual-communal dialectic regarding the discernment of the Spirit via accentuating the church as the people of God (see *Lumen Gentium* # 9); via the affirmation of the trifold dignity of baptism—by baptism all are made sharers in the priestly, prophetic and kingly ministry of Jesus (see *Lumen Gentium* #31); via its advocacy of ministerial leadership that is deferential toward and consultative of the laity so as to advance the laity's participation in ecclesial decision-making processes (see *Lumen Gentium* #'s 12 and 37); via advocating subsidiarity; and via its anthropological affirmation of the primary dignity of the human person residing in one's conscience (see above).

By their very nature, theology and church teaching deal with mysteries and the complexities of living a life expressing the gospel values. As such, theology and church teaching are not matters of solving problems but, rather, invitations to perennial and perpetual discernment as the faithful strive to ascertain how to live out the faith. More than a deontological enterprise, the Catholic vision of Christian life is one of relationships—with God, others and the ecclesial community. Hence, diaconal ministry and counseling ought to be marked by relationship building via love.

Additionally, the Christian faith is catholic—universal—allowing for diverse and pluralistic expressions. Such diversity and pluralism of expression is rooted in the fact that the faith is also apostolic (e.g., diversity of gospel expressions and moral guidance proffered in the New Testament). Precisely as apostolic, Christian theology and tradition are marked by diversity and pluralism. Consequently, the hallmark of diaconal ministry and counseling ought to be humility, i.e., a disposition open to divergent expressions, and slow to presume uniformity.

Deacons are ones who have been fortunate to have experienced a formation process rich in theological and ecclesial formation. Therefore, their ministry is one of stewardship vis-à-vis these treasures of the faith. Responsible stewardship requires that one share this treasure in a manner that respects the diverse and pluralistic expression of truth, tradition and ecclesial teaching, which are their very characteristics. Consequently, diaconal ministry/counseling ought to be marked by sharing this reality with those who are served in a manner that is respectful of and true to them as distinct persons, as well as to the very nature of truth, tradition and church teaching. As stewards of these treasures, a deacon's task becomes one of inviting others into the diverse and pluralistic expressions of the faith as they strive to discern how best to give it expression in their own lives. When a deacon exercises ministry in this manner he models the ministry/counseling of Jesus as described above. Above all, the ministerial example of Jesus was one characterized by service—service which, in turn, is characterized by love (see Matthew 20:25–28 and John 13).

Such a pastoral disposition calls for sensitivity, empathy, patience, temperance and the realization that living the moral life is not a matter of adhering to moral absolutes but, rather, a life-long process of *metanoi*—conversion and reconciliation. In his apostolic exhortation on *Reconciliation and Penance in the World Today* (*Reconciliatio et Paenitentia*), the late pope, John Paul II, described the moral dynamic as follows:

> . . . metanoia . . . means the inmost change of the heart under the influence of the word of God and in the perspective of the kingdom . . . the concrete daily effort of a person, supported by God's grace . . . that passes from the heart to . . . the Christian's whole life. (*Reconciliatio et Paenitentia* #4)

Contemporary moral theology describes the pastoral approach being described as a relational-responsibility model.[28] Paul Tillich noted that all theology is situational, i.e., born out of the personal situation and the context out of which one's existential questions and reception of church teachings arise. These factors include one's self-awareness, freedom, space, power and competency. Collectively, these shape and color one's attempts to in-

---

28. Gula, *Reason Informed by Faith*, 21 and 304–6.

terpret and apply moral teachings and are done so, furthermore, within the context of one's own particular religious experience and in light of the issues and concerns of one's particular historical time. Thus, if moral deliberation is situational/contextual, so must be pastoral ministry and counseling. Therefore, ministerial counseling must be relational—meeting the person where they are at—and proffered in light of the others' context/situation. Rather than seeing the moral life as a matter of standing alone before a pre-arranged system of rules, the relational-responsible approach sees the moral life as a matter of ongoing relationships with God and others. The moral theologian, Richard Gula, SS, describes the relational-responsibility model this way:

> It recognizes the uniqueness of all standpoints, considers an action as part of an ongoing set of interactions, and emphasizes the ongoing process of relationships which make up the context.[29]

This model understands that moral meaning is to be discovered within a relational context and acknowledges that an individual can discover moral meaning, and empowers them to do so. When this happens, conversion results, i.e., a moral life embraced experientially rather than via imposition from an external authority. When the moral life emerges in this manner, it emerges out of one's character which, in turn, will continue to inform their moral discernment and sense of virtue in future contexts. The best way a deacon can shape the character of those whom he serves is by sharing the stories, symbols and rituals of the faith which invite relationship with God and one another.

Hence, diaconal pastoral guidance ought to address the particular person in their immediate situation and be open to the gradualness of moral maturation. A deacon's pastoral posture ought to be marked by an openness to understand the other person's history, values and limited capacities. The critical dimension of this posture ought to be prophetic, not punitive, i.e., sharing the Christian message so as to illuminate the good toward which

29. Ibid., 304.

one ought to strive. This does not mean that the deacon abandon accepted communal normative moral standards, rather the deacon is called to hold in tension the objective norms of morality vis-à-vis a particular person's capacity for moral responsibility. Again, in the words of Gula:

> From within this framework the challenge to the pastoral person is to be true to both the objective norms of morality (such as we find expressed in the moral teaching of the magisterium) and at the same time to be respectful of the limited, subjective capacities of the person to embody the values upheld by these norms.[30]

A deacon's pastoral procedures ought to clarify, confront, proffer images which illuminate conversion, and explore alternatives. Ministering in this manner, again, calls upon deacons to be mindful of the processional nature of the moral life as well as the impediments impacting the person before them. While employing a relational-responsibility model of pastoral counseling, deacons must avoid two extremes: 1) uncompromising enforcement of normative standards in a manner which suggests that the standard captures the whole of truth and thus dictates what must be done regardless of the person's capacities (such an approach fails to honor the complex, diverse and pluralistic nature of truth, and also fails to acknowledge the conditionality of human articulations of moral standards); 2) allowing sentiment to serve as the exhaustive expression of moral truth, determining what is to be done devoid of concern for wider relational impacts. Avoiding said extremes, in turn, ensures that the extremes of legalistic idolatry and moral relativism are, likewise, avoided.

---

30. Ibid., 307.

# 6

# Pope Francis and Vatican II's
# Vision of Church

## *Implications for Deacons*

### The Church's Missionary Impulse

LIKE THE SECOND VATICAN Council, Pope Francis has inspired new life and vitality within the Roman Catholic Church. He has done so, just as the council did, by calling upon the church to share the joy of the gospel and an encounter with Jesus in ever new ways (see *Evangelii Gaudium* #'s 11–12). At the heart of the pope's call to a new evangelization are joy and mercy. No one is to be excluded from joy and mercy for Jesus wishes to share himself with each and all, and God never tires of forgiving (see *Evangelii Gaudium* #'s 1 and 3). Therefore, the church must go forth to everyone without exception, especially the poor, sick, despised and overlooked (see *Evangelii Gaudium* #'s 48, 113, 114). Toward this end, Pope Francis prefers that the church be bruised, dirty and hurting as a result of it being out at the service of others (see *Evangelii Gaudium* #49).

Just as Pope John XXIII had wished to throw open the doors of the church and for the church to go out to the world therefrom, Pope Francis desires the same for the church by inviting the faithful not to fear going astray nor be shut up within ecclesial structures or a sense of *ad intra* security afforded by ecclesial rules and habits but, rather, to live out one's faith *ad extra* in service to others (see *Evangelii Gaudium* #49). As recipients of God's infinite love, the church ought to seek ways and means to share this love with others by committing herself to growing in her interpretations of revelation and understanding of truth which she receives in inexhaustible variety (see *Evangelii Gaudium* #'s 6, 10, 40). Indeed, Pope Francis maintains that doctrinal, moral and pastoral issues can be interpreted in light of regional and cultural traditions and needs so as to ensure the church's efficacy (see *Amoris Laetitia* #'s 3, 199, 248).

> Unity of teaching and practice is certainly necessary in the church, but this does not preclude various ways of interpreting some aspects of that teaching or drawing certain consequences from it. This will always be the case as the Spirit guides us . . . Each country or region, moreover, can seek solutions better suited to its culture and sensitive to its traditions and local needs. (*Amoris Latitia* #3)

The church accomplishes this by reaching out to others and working for their good (see *Evangelii Gaudium* #9). Therefore, the church must go forth.

The church must take part in a missionary going forth that calls her out of her comfort zone in order to reach all people on the peripheries so that the gospel can be heard and Jesus encountered (see *Evangelii Gaudium* #20). Such a missionary impulse demands a kind of *kenosis* on part of the church as the church respects the unpredictable nature of the Spirit's impulse and which excludes no one (see *Evangelii Gaudium* #'s 22–23). The church, as an evangelizing community, must work for solidarity among peoples, abase itself if necessary, and embrace the suffering of people and take on "the smell of the sheep". In this regard, Pope Francis has likened the church to a field hospital. The church must accompany people where they are and exercise patience as the Spirit illuminates new ways for the joy of the gospel to take flesh in particular situations and bear new fruits of life amongst people (see *Evangelii Gaudium* #24). Echoing the Second Vatican Council's identification of the church as a missionary servant at pilgrimage amongst all peoples seeking to read the signs of the times so as to discover new ways and means for the Truths of the gospel (big-"T" Truths) to be communicated in ways that are intelligible, meaningful, relevant, viable and life-giving to all persons (little-"t" truths), Pope Francis has stated:

> I dream of a . . . missionary impulse capable of transforming everything so that the church's customs, ways of doing things, times and schedules, language and structures, can be suitably channeled for the evangelization of today's world rather than for the church's self-preservation. (*Evangelii Gaudium* #27)

> . . . today's vast and rapid cultural changes demand that we constantly seek ways of expressing unchanging truths [Big "T's"] in language which brings out their abiding newness [little "t's"]. The deposit of the faith is one thing [big "T"] . . . the way it is expressed is another [little "t's"] . . . Let us never forget that the expression of truth can take different forms. The renewal of these forms of expression becomes necessary for the sake of transmitting to the people of today the Gospel message in its unchanging meaning. (*Evangelii Gaudium* # 41)

Like the Second Vatican Council, Pope Francis calls for the church to read the signs of the times so as to interpret them in light of the gospel, thereby ensuring that the church serves as a sacrament unto the world.

## Pope Francis: A Model of *Diakonia* and *Kenosis*

Via his own lived example and via the manner and way which he exercises the papal office, Francis has evidenced the kind of *kenosis* and missionary orientation espoused by the Second Vatican Council. Echoing the teachings of the council, the pope's message is constantly one of being open to the world, being open to ecclesial *kenosis*, change and cultural adaption. His message is also constantly marked by an accent upon the love and mercy of

God which is the joy of the gospel. His apostolic exhortation, *The Joy of the Gospel* (*Evangelii Gaudium*), reads like a synopsis of the sixteen documents promulgated by the Second Vatican Council as it calls for a new missionary impulse within the church marked by Spirit-filled evangelizers who go forth unto the world to share the message of God's love and mercy to all human beings . . . and to do so in ways and means that are marked by joy, inclusion and non-judgment. The pope calls for the church to be humble as it recognizes God's presence and the work of the Spirit inherent in the lives of all people. Like the council, the pope posits that renewed and reformed expressions (little "t's") of the gospel Truths (Big "T's") are to be the means for the church's missionary success. Commitment to the anthropological, Christological and Pneumatological vision of the Christian faith, coupled with living out the principles of Catholic Social Teaching, continue to be means by which the church can successfully evangelize and anticipate God's kingdom on earth.

Not only via his message has Pope Francis given renewed impetus and life to the ecclesiological vision of the Second Vatican Council, but also via his lived witness. Like Pope John XXIII, Pope Francis has a pastor's heart. Reports frequently indicate that the pope goes forth from the Vatican to minister to the poor, homeless, hungry, disfigured and imprisoned. His priestly actions have witnessed examples of interreligious inclusion as he has washed the feet of non-Christians and respected the consciences of married couples in interreligious unions. He has witnessed great compassion toward and a desire to better understand the LGTBQ community and those who have suffered a divorce. His pastoral ministry and counseling has been inclusive as well, as he has frequently warned against excessive dogmatism and being too judgmental.

> . . . the first proclamation must ring out over and over: Jesus Christ loves you . . . stressing . . . God's saving love which precedes any moral and religious obligation . . . it should not impose the truth but appeal to freedom; it should be marked by joy, encouragement . . . not reduced to a few doctrines . . . All this demands on the part of the

evangelizer certain attitudes which foster openness to the message: approachability, readiness for dialogue, patience, a warmth and welcome which is non-judgmental. (*Evangelii Gaudium* #'s 64–65)

The focus of his ministry has been what he teaches, i.e., going forth promoting and fostering interpersonal relationships between the Lord and the people whom he serves. Mean spirited theology and utilizing the faith as a weapon and/or in punitive ways is foreign to the example of Pope Francis. "What counts above all else is faith working through love . . . Being a disciple means being constantly ready to bring the love of Jesus to others . . ." (*Evangelii Gaudium* #'s 37 and 127).

True to his call for universality and inculturation, Francis has also exercised his papal ministry in a manner that *kenotically* decentralizes certain ecclesial decision-making by calling upon bishops, synods and episcopal conferences to discern and implement decisions which resonate with the lived experiences of the people to whom they minister. With incredible humility, the pope speaks of not looking to the papacy for all ecclesial decisions, trusting that the Spirit is, indeed, at work among the laity and other members of the hierarchy. The pope has confidence that his brother bishops and the laity to whom they minister are capable, with the Spirit's guidance, of discerning what is required and what is best for meeting the pastoral needs of their ecclesial communities. Additionally, the pope's leadership style reflects a confidence that ecclesial unity can, indeed, be maintained even in the midst of diversity and plurality when it comes to the faith in praxis.

From the time of Pope Alexander V (1447–1455 CE), the pope's private chapel in the Vatican has been adorned by paintings proffered by the Dominican friar Fra Angelico. These paintings which surround the pope during his times of personal prayer are comprised of scenes from the lives of the church's early deacons— saints Stephen and Lawrence. These early deacons, like the pope's namesake Francis of Assisi, were animated by the Spirit to go forth unto the world so as to proclaim the gospel and evidenced that the poor were, indeed, the treasures of the church. Francis has, seemingly, been inspired by the example of these deacons and, in turn, can serve to inspire deacons today. A deacon would do well to emulate the theological, ministerial, pastoral, homiletic and lived witness of Pope Francis. By modeling the ministry of Pope Francis deacons would do much to actualize Vatican II's vision and contribute much to the making of a servant church.

## Spirit-Filled Evangelizers

As Vatican II foresaw, the pope suggests that a church thus missionary disposed will require that lay people, who constitute parishes, will have to exhibit flexibility and adaptability as the church strives to inculturate itself amongst the lived experiences of people, especially persons on the outskirts and in diverse sociocultural settings (see *Evangelii Gaudium #*'s 28 and 30).

> It is imperative . . . to inculturate the Gospel . . . What is called for is an evangelization capable of shedding light on new ways of relating to God, to others and the world around us, and inspiring essential values. (*Evangelii Gaudium #*'s 69 and 74; see also #'s 115 and 122)

> The church . . . needs to grow in her interpretation of the revealed word and in her understanding of truth . . . today's vast and rapid cultural changes demand that we constantly seek ways of expressing . . . truths in a language which brings about their abiding newness . . . Let us never forget that the expression of truth can take different forms. The renewal of these forms of expression becomes necessary for the sake of transmitting to the people of today the Gospel message . . . (*Evangelii Gaudium #*'s 40–41)

> We should not think that the Gospel message must always be communicated by fixed formulations learned by heart or by specific words which express an absolutely invariable content. (*Evangelii Gaudium* #129)

Inculturation respects that there is no single cultural expression of the faith and that cultural diversity and plurality serve the church's catholicity for every culture assists the church in providing values and norms whereby the gospel can be more effectively preached, understood and lived (see *Evangelii Gaudium* #'s 116–18).

> Whenever we make the effort to return to the source and to recover the original freshness of the Gospel, new avenues arise, new paths of creativity open up, with different forms of expression, more eloquent signs and words with new meaning for today's world. (*Evangelii Gaudium* #11)

Ecclesial unity need not necessitate or require uniformity and "it is an indisputable fact that no single culture can exhaust the mystery of redemption in Christ" (*Evangelii Gaudium* #118).

> . . . God's gift becomes flesh in the culture of those who receive it . . . The history of Christianity shows that Christianity does not have simply one cultural expression . . . in accordance with cultures . . . the Holy Spirit . . . shows her new aspects of revelation . . . every culture offers positive values and forms which can enrich the way the Gospel is preached, understood and lived. (*Evangelii Gaudium* #'s 115–16)

Francis, again like Vatican II, calls upon bishops to foster this missionary impulse of the church by allowing the laity to strike out on new paths and by creating a dynamic and open ecclesial communion wherein means of lay participation are developed and encouraged (see *Evangelii Gaudium* #31). Like Vatican II, Pope Francis deems every Christian a missionary (see *Evangelii Gaudium* #120).

> Lay people are, put simply, the vast majority of the people of God. The minority—ordained ministers of God are at their service . . . Being Church means being God's people . . . God's leaven in the midst of humanity. (*Evangelii Gaudium* #'s 102 and 114)

The pope has reaffirmed the responsibilities and sacramental dignity of the laity taught by the Second Vatican Council and laments that more room for them to speak, act and share in ecclesial decision-making has been impeded by excessive clericalism, especially in regards to women in the church (see *Evangelii Gaudium* #'s 102–3).

> In all of the baptized from first to last, the sanctifying power of the Spirit is at work impelling us to evangelization . . . In virtue of their baptism, all members of the People of God have become missionary disciples. All the baptized, whatever their position within the Church or their level of instruction in the faith, are agents of evangelization. (*Evangelii Gaudium* #'s 119 and 120)

He has acknowledged the Spirit's sanctifying power at work amongst the laity and their infallibility in matters of belief, just as Vatican II spoke of the laity's prophetic baptismal dignity and role within the Magisterium as the *sensus fidei* (see *Evangelii Gaudium* #119).

> Every Christian is a missionary . . . each of us should find ways to communicate Jesus wherever we are . . . The Holy Spirit enriches the entire evangelizing Church with different charisms. These gifts are meant to renew and build up the Church. (*Evangelii Gaudium* #'s 120–21 and 130)

> As part of his mysterious love for humanity God furnishes the totality of the faithful with an instinct of faith—sensus fidei . . . (*Evangelii Gaudium* # 120)

Consistent with Vatican II's call for the church to be a sacrament of Jesus unto the world, Pope Francis deems faith working through love directed to others as the most perfect manifestation of the church's interior graces afforded by the Spirit (see *Evangelii Gaudium* #37). Love before all else is to guide the church's efforts and ought never be obscured (see *Evangelii Gaudium* #39). In the church's efforts to manifest love to others, she may have to come to see that certain customs and practices of deep historical roots may no longer be understood and appreciated and, thus, no longer suitable means for communicating the gospel or shaping the lives of people (see *Evangelii Gaudium* #43). Therefore, in an act of *kenosis*, the church may have to let the aforesaid go.

> . . . the Church can also come to see that certain customs not directly related to the heart of the Gospel . . . are no

longer properly understood and appreciated. Some of these customs may be beautiful, but they no longer serve as a means of communicating the Gospel. We should not be afraid to re-examine them. (*Evangelii Gaudium* #43)

Given their position within the church and their level of instruction and formation in the faith, deacons are able to be agents of evangelization in ways and means unique to their vocation, their membership in the church's hierarchy and informed by their lived situations, therefore they should heed the pope's call to be bold in communicating Jesus where they are and to afford others an explicit witness of the saving love of Jesus (see *Evangelii Gaudium* #'s 33 and 120–21). As discussed throughout this book, the ministries and lives of deacons situate them within historical-existential contexts similar to and which parallel those of the lay faithful. Therefore, deacons are in contact with the underlying popular piety of those whom they serve. Pope Francis recognizes that there is an *active evangelizing power* inherent in the said popular piety which the church ought not underestimate but, rather, tap into so as to honor the work of the Holy Spirit in the lives of the faithful so as to promote and strengthen it (see *Evangelii Gaudium* #125). Just as deacons can do much to facilitate the baptismal dignity and social apostolates of the laity (see previous chapters), so, too, can they do much to promote the popular piety of those whom they serve and allow said pietistic tendencies to shape, color and inform their diaconal ministries and preaching so that their ministries and message resonate with the lived experiences of the people in ways that are intelligible, relevant, meaningful and live-giving.

## Joyfully and Compassionately Proclaiming God's Mercy to All

In their preaching, deacons should heed the instructions of Pope Francis and be humble, respectful and gentle, inviting the faithful into an interpersonal dialogue in which the love of God is always the fundamental message (see *Evangelii Gaudium* #128).

> Being a disciple means being constantly ready to bring
> the love of Jesus to others, and this can happen unex-
> pectedly and in any place . . . In this preaching, which
> is always respectful and gentle, the first step is personal
> dialogue . . . always keeping in mind the fundamental
> message: the personal love of God . . . This message is
> to be shared humbly . . . (*Evangelii Gaudium* #'s 127–28)

Respectful of the experiences and cultural context of those whom
they serve, deacons should keep in mind that the gospel message
need not be tied to fixed formulations, specific words or absolute
and invariable content, but, rather, communicated in diverse and
pluralistic ways respectful of cultural diversity, historical processes
and the experiences of the faithful so as to ensure that the gospel
message does not stagnate nor become something offered only to
a small group (see *Evangelii Gaudium* #'s 128–30).

> God always invites us to take a step forward, but does
> not demand a full response if we are not yet ready . . .
> The preacher needs to keep his ear to the people and to
> discover what it is that the faithful need to hear . . . He
> needs to be able to link the message of a biblical text to
> a human situation . . . What we are looking for is what
> the Lord has to say in this or that particular situation.
> (*Evangelii Gaudium* #'s 153–54)

The challenge of inculturated preaching, according to the pope, is
a synthesis between God's message and the life of the hearers, for
the task of the preacher is to join the hearts of God with the hearts
of the people so as to strengthen the covenantal bond between
them and to inspire charity (see *Evangelii Gaudium* #143). Effective proclamation of the gospel requires deacons to be conversant
with contemporary scientific, professional and academic findings
in order to ensure that the credibility of the faith remains sound
and that the content of the church's teachings effectively bear
upon the contemporary lived experiences of people (see *Evangelii
Gaudium* #'s 132–33). In short, a deacon's homily ought to echo
a mother's discourse to her children, i.e., marked by love, trust,
intimacy, joy, acknowledgment of God's work within the hearers,

guided by the Spirit, directed beyond the weaknesses of the hearer and aimed towards the good of the hearer (see *Evangelii Gaudium* #'s 139–41). If a deacon wishes to adapt to the people and reach them with God's word, he needs to share in their lives and pay loving attention to them (see *Evangelii Gaudium* #158)

As ordained members of the hierarchy entrusted with the privilege and responsibility of offering homilies to the faithful, deacons do well to consider the pope's reminder that the homily is an important aspect of ordained ministry for it serves as a kind of touchstone of the closeness between the clergy and the faithful and is key to the clergy's communication with the people (see *Evangelii Gaudium* #135). Furthermore, God reaches out to others through those who have the charism of preaching so that a dialogue between God and the people may occur (see *Evangelii Gaudium* #136). As an expression of God's word to the people conducted within the context of the Eucharist, the homily mediates grace and fosters communion (see *Evangelii Gaudium* #'s 137–38).

> It is worth remembering that the liturgical proclamation of the word of God . . . is not so much a time for meditation and catechesis as a dialogue between God and His people . . . it is a part of the offering made to the Father and a mediation of the grace which Christ pours out during the celebration. (*Evangelii Gaudium* # 138)

Therefore, deacons ought to prepare for preaching via praying, studying and reflecting, for, according to Francis, "a preacher who does not prepare is not spiritual; he is dishonest and irresponsible with the gifts he has received" (*Evangelii Gaudium* #'s 145 and 152–53). Preparing to preach requires love, humility and reverence for God's truth which is always beyond us. A deacon needs to respect that he is not the master or owner of God's word, but is its herald and servant (see *Evangelii Gaudium* #146). Comprehending the meaning of God's word, contextualizing God's word within the broader teachings of the church, and personalizing what is preached are requisite for effective preaching so that God's love always has the last word (see *Evangelii Gaudium* #'s 147–50). Therefore, preaching ought to be positive and aimed at the hearer's growth in faith and love for others (see *Evangelii Gaudium* #'s 159–60).

> Another feature of a good homily is that it is positive. It is not so much concerned with pointing out what shouldn't be done, but with suggesting what we can do better . . . Evangelization aims at a process of growth which entails taking seriously each person and God's plan for his or her life. (*Evangelii Gaudium* #s 159–60)

Diaconal teaching must also accentuate the love of God in a joyful and encouraging manner, not impose obligations nor reduce God's love to limited doctrines, i.e., diaconal teaching ought to be characterized by openness, approachability, dialogue, patience, warmth and non-judgmental welcoming (see *Evangelii Gaudium* #'s 164–65).

> . . . no one is excluded from the joy brought by the Lord . . . we are infinitely loved . . . Christians have the duty to proclaim the Gospel without excluding anyone. Instead of seeming to impose new obligations, they should appear as people who wish to share their joy . . . It is not by proselytizing that the Church grows, but by attraction. (*Evangelii Gaudium* #'s 3, 5, and 15)

> A preaching which would be purely moralistic or doctrinaire, or one which turns into a lecture . . . detracts from this heart-to-heart communication which takes place in the homily . . . (*Evangelii Gaudium* #142)

In their pastoral ministry deacons must acknowledge the myriad of challenges confronting contemporary persons, not simply decry present realities and impose rules via authority. Deacons must accompany people in the midst of these challenges and allow for the "law of gradualness" to unfold (see *Amoris Laetitia* #'s 35, 39–56, 201, 295). Pope Francis acknowledges that at times the manner of the church's teaching and pastoral counsel contributes to rather than ministers unto the concrete situations people are experiencing (see *Amoris Laetitia* #'s 36, 38). Therefore, deacons must offer understanding, comfort and acceptance, not just impose straightaway sets of rules. They must show God's mercy, not hurl stones (see *Amoris Laetitia* #'s 49, 305). Deacons ought not just lament the complex moral situations those whom they serve find themselves in but, rather, proffer a message of love and tenderness (see *Amoris Laetitia* #'s 57, 59, 207). Deacons also need to offer deference to the dignity of conscience inherent in those whom they serve and show respect for the ability of persons to respond to God as best they can within the limitations of their particular circumstances (see *Amoris Laetitia* #303). Deacons need to be mindful that they *have been called to form consciences, not to replace them* (*Amoris Laetitia* # 37). Pastoral accompaniment is to be the key hallmark of diaconal pastoral counseling (see *Amoris Laetitia* #'s 242–43, 246, 291, 293, 299–300). In short, pastoral guidance and discernment must take into account the human person (see *Amoris Laetitia* #'s 302 and 305) and be about mercy (see *Amoris Laetitia* #'s 296, 308, 310–11)!

Employing new ways of expressing truth and beauty, deacons must "be bold enough to discover new signs and new symbols, new flesh to embody and communicate the word, and different forms of beauty which are valued in different cultural settings" (*Evangelii Gaudium* #167). Additionally, joyfully disposed, deacons need to personally accompany the people they serve, offering a listening ear and open heart (see *Evangelii Gaudium* #'s 169–71).

> One who accompanies others has to realize that each person's situation before God and their life in grace are mysteries which no one can fully know from without. The Gospel tells us to correct others and to help them grow . . . without making judgments about their responsibility and culpability . . . Someone good at such accompaniment . . . invites others to be healed. (*Evangelii Gaudium* #172)

> . . . they need to accompany with mercy and patience the eventual stages of personal growth as these progressively occur . . . A missionary heart . . . never closes itself off, never retreats into its own security, never opts for rigidity and defensiveness . . . the Gospel tells us constantly to run the risk of a face-to-face encounter with others . . . The Son of God, by becoming flesh, summoned us

to the revolution of tenderness . . . Let us ask the Lord to
help us understand the law of love. (*Evangelii Gaudium*
#'s 44–45, 88, 101)

As emphasized by the Second Vatican Council, Pope Francis,
likewise, links the church's missionary evangelization with the advancement of God's kingdom in the world. Such missionary evangelization necessitates that the anthropological, Christological and
Pneumatological vision of the church be advanced universally (see
*Evangelii Gaudium* #'s 176–81) and the pope, like the council, views
the church's social teachings as central to advancing this vision . . .
*the church cannot and must not remain on the sidelines in the fight
for justice* (*Evangelii Gaudium* #183). Particularly important, the
pope advises, is the church's commitment to a preferential option
for the poor, oppressed and marginalized; solidarity; distributive
justice; the common good; peace; and environmental stewardship
(see *Evangelii Gaudium* #'s 186–241 and *Laudato Si*).

> God's heart has a special place for the poor, so much so
> that He Himself became poor . . . For the church the op-
> tion for the poor is primarily a theological category . . .
> This divine preference has consequences for the faith life
> of all Christians since we are called to have this mind of
> Christ. (*Evangelii Gaudium* #'s 197–98)

Likewise, a commitment to ecumenism and interreligious
dialogue is incumbent upon the church for such corresponds to
Jesus' prayer for the church and is indispensable to the credibility
of the church's message and her catholicity (see *Evangelii Gaudium*
#'s 244–58). As the church continues its pilgrim journey its com-
mitment to unity will prove to be indispensable to her evangelization for it will enable the church to learn from others and challenge
her to be receptive to what the Spirit is saying amongst all peoples
(see *Evangelii Gaudium* #246). Such an openness to others and to
the Spirit is a prerequisite for peace and justice in the world (see
*Evangelii Gaudium* #250).

> Commitment to ecumenism responds to the prayer
> of the Lord Jesus that "they may all be one" (Jn 17:21).

The credibility of the Christian message would be much greater if Christians could overcome their divisions and the Church could realize "the fullness of catholicity proper to her in those of her children who, though joined to her by baptism, are yet separated from full communion with her." We must never forget that we are pilgrims journeying alongside one another. This means that we must have sincere trust in our fellow pilgrims, putting aside all suspicion or mistrust, and turn our gaze to what we are all seeking: the radiant peace of God's face. (*Evangelium Gaudium* #244)

An attitude of openness in truth and in love must characterize the dialogue with the followers of non-Christian religions, in spite of various obstacles and difficulties, especially forms of fundamentalism on both sides. Interreligious dialogue is a necessary condition for peace in the world, and so it is a duty for Christians as well as other religious communities. (*Evangelium Gaudium* #250)

Just as this book has called upon deacons to be Spirit-filled evangelizers, so, too, does Pope Francis. Echoing the Second Vatican Council, the pope draws a parallel between the current church's missionary impulse with that of the post-Pentecost apostolic church (see *Evangelii Gaudium* #'s 259–61). Deacons ought to be committed to fostering friendships between those whom they serve—the people and Jesus.

To be evangelizers . . . we need to develop a spiritual taste for being close to people's lives and to discover that this itself is a source of greater joy. Mission is at once a passion for Jesus and a passion for his people . . . Jesus wants us to touch human misery, to touch the suffering flesh of others . . . Jesus does not want us to be grandees who look down upon others, but men and women of the people . . . If we are to share our lives with others and generously give of ourselves, we also have to realize that every person is worthy of our giving. (*Evangelii Gaudium* #'s 268–74)

Serving others in such a manner will, indeed, do much to make the church the servant church she is called by Jesus to be.

# Appendix

## Subsidiarity

. . . the principal of solidarity must be respected: a community of higher order should not interfere in the internal life of a community of a lower order, depriving the latter of its functions, but rather should support it in case of need . . . (Pope John Paul II, *Centesimus Annus* #48)

. . . it is a fundamental principle of social philosophy, fixed and unchangeable, that one should not withdraw from individuals and commit to the community what they can accomplish by their own enterprise and industry. So, too, it is an injustice and at the same time a grave evil and a disturbance to right order to transfer to the higher and larger collectivity functions which can be performed and provided for by lesser and subordinate bodies . . . (Pope Pius XI, *Quadragesimo Anno* #79; Pope John XXIII, *Mater et Magistra,* #53)

It is up to the Christian communities to analyze with objectivity the situation which is proper to their own country, to shed on it the light of the Gospel's unalterable words and to draw principles of reflection, norms of judgment and directives for action from the social teaching of the Church. (Pope Paul VI, *Octogesima Adveniens* #4)

## Participation/Democratic Structures

Democratic participation in decision-making is the best way to respect the dignity and liberty of people. (Pope Pius XII, *Christmas Message*, 1944)

Praise is due to those national procedures which allow the largest possible number of citizens to participate in public affairs with genuine freedom. (*Gaudium et Spes* #31)

The active participation of everyone in the running of enterprise should be promoted. (*Gaudium et Spes* #68)

For the protection of personal rights is a necessary condition for the active participation of citizens . . . (*Gaudium et Spes* #73)

It is in full accord with human nature that juridical-political structures should, with ever better success and without any discrimination, afford all their citizens the chance to participate freely and actively . . . determining the scope and purposes of various institutions, and choosing leaders. (*Gaudium et Spes* #75)

The Church values the democratic system inasmuch as it ensures the participation of its citizens in making choices, guarantees to the governed the possibility of both electing and holding accountable those who govern them, and of replacing them through peaceful means when necessary. (Pope John Paul II, *Centesimus Annus* #46)

. . . the aspiration to equality and the aspiration to participation, two forms of human dignity and freedom . . . the two aspirations seek to promote a democratic type of society. (Pope Paul VI, *Octogesima Adveniens* #22, 24)

In concrete situations, and taking account of solidarity in each person's life, one must recognize a legitimate variety of possible options. The same Christian faith can lead to different commitments. The Church invites all Christians to take up a double task of inspiring and of innovating, in order to make structures evolve, so as to adapt them to the real needs of today. (Pope Paul VI, *Octogesima Adveniens* #50)

# Bibliography

*Ad Gentes Divinitus* (*Decree on the Church's Missionary Activity*). In *Vatican Council II, Volume 1: The Conciliar and Postconciliar Documents*, edited by Austin Flannery, 813–56, New York: Costello, 1998.

*Apostolicam Actuositatem* (*Decree on the Apostolate of Lay People*). In *Vatican Council II, Volume 1: The Conciliar and Postconciliar Documents*, edited by Austin Flannery, 766–98, New York: Costello, 1998.

Baker, Thomas. "The Deacon and Work." In *The Deacon Reader*, edited by James Keating, 182–97. New York: Paulist, 2006.

Bevans, Stephen B. "*Decree on the Church's Missionary Activity* (*Ad Gentes*)." *Rediscovering Vatican II: Evangelization and Religious Freedom*. New York: Paulist, 2009.

Bevans, Stephen B., and Jeffrey Gros. *Rediscovering Vatican II: Evangelization and Religious Freedom* (*Ad Gentes, Dignitatis Humanae*). New York: Paulist, 2009.

Bonhoeffer, Dietrich. *The Cost of Discipleship*. New York: Touchstone, 1995

———. *Spiritual Care*. Translated by Jay C. Rochelle. Minneapolis: Fortress, 1985.

Borg, Marcus J. *Meeting Jesus Again for the First Time: The Historical Jesus and the Heart of Contemporary Faith*. San Francisco: Harper, 1995.

*Christus Dominus* (*Decree on the Pastoral Office of the Bishops in the Church*). In *Vatican Council II, Volume 1: The Conciliar and Postconciliar Documents*, edited by Austin Flannery, 564–90, New York: Costello, 1998.

Collins, John N. *Deacons and the Church: Making Connections between Old and New*. Harrisburg: Gracewing, 2002.

———. *Diakonia: Re-Interpreting the Ancient Sources*. New York: Oxford, 1990.

Congar, Yves. *I Believe in the Holy Spirit*. 3 vols. New York: Crossroad, 1997.

Congregation for Catholic Education. *Basic Norms for the Formation of Permanent Deacons* (*Ratio Fundamentalis Institutionis Diacononorm Permaentium*). http://www.vatican.va/roman_curia/congregations/ccatheduc/documents/rc_con_ccatheduc_doc_31031998_directorium-diaconi_en.html.

Congregation for the Clergy. *Directorium Pro Ministerio et Vita Diaconorum Permanentium* (*Directory for the Ministry and Life of Permanent Deacons*).

http://www.vatican.va/roman_curia/congregations/ccatheduc/documents/rc_con_ccatheduc_doc_31031998_directorium-diaconi_lt.html.

Cummings, Owen F. "The State of the Question." In *Theology of the Diaconate: The State of the Question*, edited by Owen F. Cummings, William T. Ditewig, and Richard R. Gaillardetz, 1–30. New York: Paulist, 2005.

Cummings, Owen F., William T. Ditewig, and Richard R. Gaillardetz, editors. *Theology of the Diaconate: The State of the Question*. New York: Paulist, 2005.

*Dei Verbum* (*Dogmatic Constitution on Divine Revelation*). In *Vatican Council II, Volume 1: The Conciliar and Postconciliar Documents*, edited by Austin Flannery, 750–65, New York: Costello, 1998.

*Dignitatis Humanae* (*Declaration on Religious Liberty*). In *Vatican Council II, Volume 1: The Conciliar and Postconciliar Documents*, edited by Austin Flannery, 799–812, New York: Costello, 1998.

———. "Vatican II and the Renewal of the Diaconate." In *The Emerging Diaconate: Servant Leaders in a Servant Church*, by William T. Ditewig, New York: Paulist, 2007.

Ditewig, William T. "Charting a Theology of the Diaconate." In *Theology of the Diaconate: The State of the Question*, edited by Owen F. Cummings, William T. Ditewig, and Richard R. Gaillardetz, 31–66. New York: Paulist, 2005.

———. "The Contemporary Renewal of the Diaconate." In *The Deacon Reader*, edited by James Keating, 27–56, New York: Paulist, 2006.

———. *The Deacon at Mass: A Theological and Pastoral Guide*. New York: Paulist, 2007.

———. *The Emerging Diaconate: Servant Leaders in a Servant Church*. New York: Paulist, 2007.

———. "The *Kenotic* Leadership of Deacons." In *The Deacon Reader*, edited by James Keating, 248–77, New York: Paulist, 2006.

———. "Vatican II and the Renewal of the Diaconate." In *The Emerging Diaconate: Servant Leaders in a Servant Church*, by William T. Ditewig, New York: Paulist, 2007.

Ditewig, William T., and Michael J. Tkacik, editors. *Forming Deacons: Ministers of Soul and Leaven*. New York: Paulist, 2010.

Donovan, William T. *The Sacrament of Service: Understanding Diaconal Spirituality*. Green Bay: Alt, 2000.

Doyle, Dennis. *The Church Emerging from Vatican II*. Mystic: Twenty-Third, 2002.

Dulles, Avery. *Models of the Church*. New York: Doubleday, 2002.

Edward J. Enright. "The History of the Diaconate." In *The Deacon Reader*, edited by James Keating, 7–26, New York: Paulist, 2006.

*Eucharisticum Mysterium* (*Instruction on the Mystery of the Eucharist*). In *Vatican Council II, Volume 1: The Conciliar and Postconciliar Documents*, edited by Austin Flannery, 100–136, New York: Costello, 1998.

Flannery, Austin, editor. *Vatican Council II, Volume I: The Conciliar and Post Conciliar Documents*. New York: Costello, 1998.

Francis, Pope. *Amoris Laetitia* (*The Joy of Love*). Maryland: Word Among Us, 2016.

———. *Laudato Si* (*On Care for Our Common Home*). Maryland: Word Among Us, 2015.

———. *Evangelii Gaudium* (*The Joy of the Gospel*). Maryland: Word Among Us, 2013.

Gaillardetz, Richard R. "On the Theological Integrity of the Diaconate." In *Theology of the Diaconate: The State of the Question*, edited by Owen F. Cummings, William T. Ditewig, and Richard R. Gaillardetz, 67–97. New York: Paulist, 2005.

Gaillardetz, Richard R., and Catherine E. Clifford. *Keys to the Council: Unlocking the Teaching of Vatican II*. Collegeville, MN: Liturgical, 2012.

*Gaudium et Spes* (*Pastoral Constitution on the Church in the Modern World*). In *Vatican Council II, Volume 1: The Conciliar and Postconciliar Documents*, edited by Austin Flannery, 903–1001. New York: Costello, 1998.

*Gravissimum Educationis* (*Declaration on Christian Education*). In *Vatican Council II, Volume 1: The Conciliar and Postconciliar Documents*, edited by Austin Flannery, 725–37, New York: Costello, 1998.

Gula, Richard M. *Reason Informed by Faith: Foundations of Catholic Morality*. New York: Paulist, 1989.

Hanigan, James P. *As I Have Loved You: The Challenge of Christian Ethics*. New York: Paulist, 1986.

Hughes, Alfred C., Fredercik F. Campbell, and William T. Ditewig, editors. *Today's Deacon: Contemporary Issues and Cross-Currents*. New York: Paulist, 2006.

John XXIII, Pope. *Humanae Salutis* (*Apostolic Constitution Convoking the Second Vatican Council*). December 25, 1961. English translation at https://jakomonchak.files.wordpress.com/2011/12/humanae-salutis.pdf.

———. "Opening Address of the Second Vatican Council." http://www.ourladyswarriors.org/teach/v2open.htm.

———. "Opening Prayer for the Second Vatican Council." https://www.rockforddiocese.org/pdfs/parishplanning/opening_prayer.pdf.

———. *Pacem in Terris* (*Peace on Earth*). http://w2.vatican.va/content/john-xxiii/en/encyclicals/documents/hf_j-xxiii_enc_11041963_pacem.html.

John Paul II, Pope. *Centesimus Annus On the Hundredth Anniversary of Rerum Novarum*. https://w2.vatican.va/content/john-paul-ii/en/encyclicals/documents/hf_jp-ii_enc_01051991_centesimus-annus.html.

———. "Deacon Has Many Pastoral Functions." http://www.ewtn.com/library/papaldoc/jp931013.htm.

———. "Deacons Serve the Kingdom of God." http://www.ewtn.com/library/PAPALDOC/JP931005.htm.

———. *Dives in Misericordia* (*Rich in Mercy*). http://w2.vatican.va/content/john-paul-ii/en/encyclicals/documents/hf_jp-ii_enc_30111980_dives-in-misericordia.html.

———. *Dominum et Vivicantem* (*On the Holy Spirit in the Life of the Church and the World*). http://w2.vatican.va/content/john-paul-ii/en/encyclicals/documents/hf_jp-ii_enc_18051986_dominum-et-vivificantem.html.

———. *Ex Corde Ecclesia* (*On Catholic Universities*). http://w2.vatican.va/content/john-paul-ii/en/apost_constitutions/documents/hf_jp-ii_apc_15081990_ex-corde-ecclesiae.html.

———. "The Heart of the Diaconate: Servants of the Mysteries of Christ and Servant of Your Brothers and Sisters." http://www.diakonoskorner.org/Resources/Files/ADUS.pdf. Also: http://w2.vatican.va/content/john-paul-ii/en/speeches/1987/september/documents/hf_jp-ii_spe_19870919_diaconi-permanenti-detroit.html.

———. *Reconciliatio et Paenitentia* (*Reconciliation and Penance in the Mission of the Church Today*). Boston: St. Paul, 1984.

———. *Tertio Millennio Adveniente* (*For the Jubilee Year 2000*). https://w2.vatican.va/content/john-paul-ii/en/apost_letters/1994/documents/hf_jp-ii_apl_19941110_tertio-millennio-adveniente.html.

———. *Ut Unum Sint* (*On Commitment to Ecumenism*). http://w2.vatican.va/content/john-paul-ii/en/encyclicals/documents/hf_jp-ii_enc_25051995_ut-unum-sint.html.

Keating, James, editor. *The Deacon Reader*. New York: Paulist, 2006.

———. *The Heart of the Diaconate: Communion with the Servant Mysteries of Christ*. New York: Paulist, 2015.

———. "The Moral Life of the Deacon." In *The Deacon Reader*, edited by James Keating, 78–98, New York: Paulist, 2006.

*Liturgiae Instaurationes* (*The Instruction on the Correct Implementation of the Constitution on the Sacred Liturgy*). In *Vatican Council II, Volume 1: The Conciliar and Postconciliar Documents*, edited by Austin Flannery, 209–221, New York: Costello, 1998.

*Lumen Gentium* (*Dogmatic Constitution on the Church*). In *Vatican Council II, Volume 1: The Conciliar and Postconciliar Documents*, edited by Austin Flannery, 350–426, New York: Costello, 1998.

McKnight, William S. "The Diaconate as *Medius Ordo*: Service in Promotion of Lay Participation." In *The Deacon Reader*, edited by James Keating, 78–98, New York: Paulist, 2006.

McPartlan, Paul. "The Deacon and *Gaudium et Spes*." In *The Deacon Reader*, edited by James Keating, 56–77. New York: Paulist, 2006.

Noll, Ray R. "The Sacramental Ministry of the Deacon in Parish Life." In *The Deacon Reader*, edited by James Keating, 198–210, New York: Paulist, 2006.

*Nostra Aetate* (*Declaration on the Relations of the Church to Non-Christian Religions*). In *Vatican Council II, Volume 1: The Conciliar and Postconciliar Documents*, edited by Austin Flannery, 738–42, New York: Costello, 1998.

Osborne, Kenan B. *The Permanent Diaconate: Its History and Place in the Sacrament of Orders*. New York: Paulist, 2007.

Paul VI, Pope. *Ad Pascendum*. http://diaconate-form.blogspot.com/2012/05/ad-pascendum-english-translation.html.

———. "Address to the United Nations." https://w2.vatican.va/content/paul-vi/en/speeches/1965/documents/hf_p-vi_spe_19651004_united-nations.html.

———. "Homily at the Last General Session of Vatican II." http://w2.vatican.va/content/paul-vi/en/speeches/1965/documents/hf_p-vi_spe_19651207_epilogo-concilio.html.

———. *Octogesima Adveniens (On the 80th Anniversary of Rerum Novarum)*. http://w2.vatican.va/content/paul-vi/en/apost_letters/documents/hf_p-vi_apl_19710514_octogesima-adveniens.html

———. *Sacrum Diaconatus Ordinem (General Norms for Restoring the Permanent Diaconate in the Latin Church)*. http://w2.vatican.va/content/paul-vi/en/motu_proprio/documents/hf_p-vi_motu-proprio_19670618_sacrum-iaconatus.html.

Pius XI, Pope. *Quadragesimo Anno (On Reconstruction of the Social Order)*. http://w2.vatican.va/content/pius-xi/en/encyclicals/documents/hf_p-xi_enc_19310515_quadragesimo-anno.html.

Pius XII, Pope. "Christmas Message 1944." http://www.papalencyclicals.net/pius12/p12xmas.htm.

*Presbyterorum Ordinis (Decree on the Ministry and Life of Priests)*. In *Vatican Council II, Volume 1: The Conciliar and Postconciliar Documents*, edited by Austin Flannery, 863–902, New York: Costello, 1998.

Richard, Lucien. "Vatican II and the Mission of the Church: A Contemporary Agenda." In *Vatican II: The Unfinished Agenda—A Look to the Future*, edited by Lucien Richard, Daniel Harrington, and John W. O'Malley, 57–70, New York: Paulist, 1987.

Richard, Lucien, Daniel Harrington, and John W. O'Malley, editors. *Vatican II: The Unfinished Agenda—A Look to the Future*. New York: Paulist, 1987.

Ross, Michael. "The Deacon: Icon of the Sign of Hope." In *The Deacon Reader*, edited by James Keating, 99–118, New York: Paulist, 2006.

*Sacrosanctum Concilium (The Constitution on the Sacred Liturgy)*. In *Vatican Council II, Volume 1: The Conciliar and Postconciliar Documents*, edited by Austin Flannery, 1–36, New York: Costello, 1998.

Schillebeeckx, Edward. *Christ the Sacrament of the Encounter with God*. New York: Sheed and Ward, 1963.

Tkacik, Michael J., and Thomas C. McGonigle. *Pneumatic Correctives: What Is the Spirit Saying to the Church of the Twenty-First Century?* Lanham, MD: University Press of America, 2007.

*Unitatis Redintegratio (Decree on Ecumenism)*. In *Vatican Council II, Volume 1: The Conciliar and Postconciliar Documents*, edited by Austin Flannery, 452–70, New York: Costello, 1998.

United States Conference of Catholic Bishops. *Called and Gifted: The American Catholic Laity*. Washington, DC: United States Conference of Catholic Bishops, 1980.

———. *Fulfilled in Your Hearing: The Homily in the Sunday Assembly*. Washington, DC: USCCB, 1982.

———. *National Directory for the Formation, Ministry and Life of Permanent Deacons in the United States*. Washington, DC: USCCB, 2005.

———. *To Teach as Jesus Did: A Pastoral Message on Catholic Education*. Washington, DC: USCCB, 1972.

Untener, Ken. *Preaching Better: Practical Suggestions for Homilists*. New York: Paulist, 1999.

Waznak, Robert P. *An Introduction to the Homily*. Collegeville, MN: Liturgical, 1998.